DISCIPLINE-
AN ACT OF LOVE

A LOVING RELATIONSHIP
WITH YOUR CHILD

By Dr. Emilie Van Wyk

ISBN: 9798377401568

THIS BOOK IS LOVINGLY

DEDICATED TO:

My husband Gerhard Van Wyk,
Our Children
Charl, Faith and Joseph,
Nadine and Stephen, and
All the teachers and students of Presda Primary school
from 1981-1999

CONTENTS

ACKNOWLEDGEMENTS

My deepest thanks and appreciation to the following people:

My mother Margareta (Feistel) Müller, who raised us with much love and dedication. She instilled in us the worth and value of people and through her positive guidance and unselfish love she guided us to love God and His Word.

Dr. Gerhard Van Wyk, my husband, for his wisdom and expertise that he shared with me. Also, his constructive suggestions and recommendations are sincerely appreciated. I also wish to thank him for his love, support and encouragement through all these 57 years.

Dr. Charl Van Wyk, our son and his wife, Dr. Faith Lukens for their encouraging interest and support always. Thank you for sharing little Joseph, your most precious possession with us, so that we could love, learn and experience him growing up. Thank you for assisting me with the printing.

Dr. Nadine Van Wyk, our daughter and her husband, Stephen LeBarre for your interest, recommendations and encouraging support at all times. Your positive suggestions and help are sincerely appreciated. Thank you for your willingness to read through the book and give me advice.

Janet Borisevich for her hard, capable, thorough, and professional way of editing this book. Her positive guidance and willingness to assist me is sincerely appreciated.

In humbleness I sincerely thank and acknowledge my weaknesses and give my Heavenly father the glory and honor. I want to thank Him for coming to show us what love really is.

DISCIPLINE - AN ACT OF LOVE

"We are what we repeatedly do. Excellence, then, is not an act, but a habit."
Aristotle

CHAPTER 1

INTRODUCTION

God was looking for somebody who would always love Him and be loyal to Him! Somebody who could stand for the right, for truth, and goodness in an evil and sinful world. Someone who would bring up his children to listen and obey His laws. Yes, someone upon whom He could depend. God wanted to bestow a blessing on him and his children!

With God's all-seeing eye, He turned to a far city— Ur. There lived a man named Terah who had three sons: Nahor, Haran, and Abram. Abram was the youngest of the three. These boys must have had a very devoted mother. She probably took special time to tell her children all about their Creator and the Creation story and God's wonderful love for Adam and Eve and all their children. She must have told them about the beginning and all the joy and glory that were theirs as they walked and talked with God. Abraham, as he was later called, learned to love the Lord, and decided that he would serve God with all his heart and be loyal to Him all of his days.

The people in Ur, as well as Abraham's father, worshiped idols. But Abraham took a firm stand for God. He would not worship idols, but only love the Lord God with all his heart. God knew he was one He could trust and with whom He could share His plan of salvation of this world.

One day, Abraham heard a voice speaking to him, and he knew at once— that this was the voice of God! God said, "Get out of this country, and go to the country which I will show you." "I will bless you and make you a great nation." God promised to make Abraham the father of many nations and through him God would bring a blessing to the whole world. God promised this, because He knew that Abraham would be an example to his children, to his servants, and his descendants. He would teach them to obey God and do what was right. They would listen to what he said and follow his example. Abraham was called the friend of God. We, who love the Lord, are all children of Abraham! We want to raise our children to listen and to love the Lord God and only worship Him who made us all.

Abraham was rich in possessions— but, most important, he was rich in faith, noble in generosity, unfaltering in obedience, and humble in simplicity of his life. He was honored by his surrounding nations as a mighty prince. His life was an example, and this was in favor of the true God. There where he lived, he was known and respected as the teacher of a new religion— a religion that serves the only true God. He always told the people about God and they could see God in his life because he lived close to the Lord and did what God wanted him to do.

". . . when I found Abraham, Isaac, and Jacob I rejoiced over them because it was like finding juicy grapes in a desert." (Hosea 9:10).

A well-ordered Christian household is a powerful argument in favor of our Christian religion. Christians can exert a mighty influence for good and be a light in this dark world. Their example can help others to guide their children to the Lord. Then, they can experience happiness that comes from the heart.

Many years passed, and then, one day, a baby boy was born in the home of Amram and Jochebed. The book of Hebrews tells us that Moses was a very special baby, and Jochebed was an exceptionally devoted mother. She hid him for three months, and then, when she could hide him no more inside the walls of their home, she made a basket and hid him in the bullrushes in the Nile River— because the king gave orders that all the babies must be killed— the Israelites had become too many in number, and they were threatening the Egyptians. They saw how God has blessed the Israelites, how they prospered, and so they became jealous of them.

Jochebed prayed to God to keep her baby safe— and God heard her prayer!

God had a plan— a very special plan for him— He sent Pharoah's daughter to go and bathe in the Nile, and there she found this precious baby— immediately, she wanted him for her very own. She ordered that he be raised by one of his people— his very own mother! God knew that she would tell him about the One and only true God.

The family thanked God for saving little Moses and now they could raise him according to the way God instructed them. She anchored his little heart to God, and carefully taught him about God, about His Creation, about Eden, and Adam and Eve, and all his descendants who were faithful to God. She made sure that he grew up to know God who created him. Those precious early twelve years were filled with the love of his parents and their God and all His wonders that surrounded him. Then, he went to live in the palace and there he learned many more vital concepts.

The book of Hebrews tells us that, when he became of age, he refused to be called the son of Pharaoh's daughter, choosing rather to suffer affliction with the people of God than to enjoy the passing pleasures of sin, because he looked to the reward— a city whose Builder and Maker is God.

Moses was a young man with unusual gifts, and he was very capable of becoming the next pharaoh. But God had better and greater plans for his life! He was a great leader and did a wonderful work for God— leading the people of Israel to the promised land!

Why is it important to raise Godly children? Proverbs 22:6 instructs us that we must train up a child in the way that they should go. It is not enough for them to try on Saul's armor to fit into— the armor they wear, the faith they are grounded in must be their own. They must be encouraged in their spiritual growth by reading the Bible to them. As they read the Bible, their brain develops more than reading any other book. Reading good books does develop the brain, but none can outsmart reading the Bible. Spend time reading the Bible with your children; make it a part of your daily routine. It 'is like oxygen to them and a firm foundation that they can stand on throughout their life.

Your children need to grasp the importance of Jesus' sacrifice for us all. They need to recognize why it is necessary to understand and accept Jesus as their personal Savior. Teach them about the Creation story— how it all began— how Adam and Eve had a relationship with God, but, because they sinned, they were separated from God. Because God is perfect, our disobedience and sin cannot stand before God's presence. But, because God still loved Adam and Eve despite their sin, He clothed them in animal skins, a symbol of how death was necessary to pay for humanity's sins, portraying a picture of the future when Christ died for our sins. For generations, people made animal sacrifices to pay for their sins, but God in His mercy sent His son to pay the price of our sins— a price that we could never pay. He conquered death and rose from the grave to restore us. Since all of us are separated from God, we must accept Jesus's gift of grace.

As your children grow, help them to understand that we cannot do anything that is enough to cover the price of our sins, and that "I'm sorry" isn't enough to cover the cost of sin— only the act of grace from Jesus dying on the cross can! Share with your child what God has done in your life— what He has brought you through— the times that He has seen you through, the places in your life that He has provided for you. You don't have to confess your sins to your child but tell them of the wonderous things He has done in your life.

Raising Godly children is an investment. It requires diligence, time, and— most importantly— you! It requires you to be an example of your faith. A child will learn more watching how you live your life and interact with people. How you spend time with God— this you could never teach them with words. To raise Godly children, our faith must be real. A child will see through what is fake. Demonstrate the faith your child should have in your daily life and habits.

The importance of passing on our faith to the next generation and raising Godly children is monumental— not to be underestimated. We have been entrusted with tomorrow's leaders of faith. They must be able to stand on their own when their faith is tested. We must pass on our faith to our children so that they will grow spiritually, becoming better acquainted with the God we serve. Psalm 78:4 says, "We will not hide from our children the things we have received but will tell them— the next generation— about the Lord's glorious power— His great deeds and the wonderful things He has done."

God has special plans for each one of us, especially in raising our gifts (children) for Him. There are many more examples in the Bible of people who raised and cared for their children to love the Lord and serve Him all of their days.

We have a very solemn responsibility as parents. We need to guide our children to God. Don't wait until they are older to decide for themselves— Satan will see to it that they do not follow the Lord who created them. It is our awesome task to guide those little feet in the path of their Creator.

1.1   Why is this important?

Why is this important when we think of discipline? The way we raise our children necessitates discipline— the practice of training in positive behavior. The way we discipline is the way they will grow up and become— and the way they will raise their children. This awesome responsibility is the greatest work we can ever do.

It is comforting to know that there are many ways to raise a child; there is not just one recipe for doing it—but all children need lots of love, care, and attention. We are all individuals, and we do things differently. No two children are alike, and no two parents are identical— this makes life interesting— and there are many experiences that influence all of us.

Somerset Maugham said: "For men and women are not only themselves, but they are also the region in which they were born, the city apartment or the farm in which they learned to walk, the games they played as children, the old wives' tales they overheard, the food they ate, the schools they attended, the sports they followed, the poems they read, and the God they believed in."

Most parents want to raise a *good* child— one who knows right from wrong, who is empathetic, and who lives by the Golden Rule. The way to raise a moral child is to be a moral person yourself. Your children will not only imitate you pushing the vacuum or washing the floors and dishes. They will also imitate the values you live by—such as faithfulness, honesty, kindness, helpfulness, and justice. Your actions are more effective than a thousand words!

Children need to grow up with sound values and beliefs. Without these values and beliefs to guide them, they will not know what they believe or who they are, and their self-image will suffer. They will not know how to make wise choices or how to live their lives. However, when they have solid Christian values and feel loved, accepted, and secure, they will make responsible choices.

Empathy is one of the first moral emotions to develop. Morality consists of not only caring for others, but also following basic rules. For example, it is never right to hurt another person. There always needs to be clear communication and a close connection between you and your child. Your relationship with your children should be central to everything you do. Be an empathetic parent and a positive model for your children. Create a loving home where your children are loved and respected— and let them know their home is a safe and wonderful place to be!

Know your children. Know who they are and what they like and dislike, realizing that they are all different. Discipline is a journey not a destination! It is a lifelong journey— It is not a technique. There is no success recipe for it; it simply is—an act of love! It is an act of love that you pour out on your children. They are the most important people in your life, and they are fearfully and wonderfully made by our Creator!

CHAPTER 2

FEARFULLY AND WONDERFULLY MADE

We are fearfully and wonderfully made! Each part of us, each organ, everything is just unimaginable. No man can make it or fully understand it! The human brain is amazing— we are fearfully and wonderfully made. It can learn, reason, and control so many automatic functions of the body. Psalm 139:14 declares, "I praise you because I am fearfully and wonderfully made; your works are wonderful, I know that full well." This verse is about the incredible nature of our physical bodies. Our bodies are the most complex and unique organism in the world! Its complexity and uniqueness speak volumes about the mind of our Creator. Every aspect of the body, down to the tiniest microscopic cell, reveals that it is fearfully and wonderfully made!

Just think— a month after conception, the tiny blood vessel which is the precursor of the heart begins to beat, and the three primary parts of the brain have already formed. Soon after that, the baby's eyes, nose, and ears start to form. By the fourth month, the unborn fetus's capacity to explore their world explodes. They can play with this umbilical cord and suck their thumbs. The structure, which is necessary for learning, has already formed!

Consider the single fertilized cell of a newly conceived human life. From that one cell within the womb develops all the different kinds of tissues, organs, and systems-- all working together at just the right time in an amazingly coordinated process. An example is the hole in the septum between the two ventricles in the heart of the newborn infant. This hole closes at exactly the right time during the birth process to allow for the oxygenation of the blood from the lungs, which does not occur while the baby is in the womb and is receiving oxygen through the umbilical cord.

We have a part to play in raising our wonderful children. You can give them a beautiful gift of a happy, healthy, and successful life by lovingly connecting with them even before they are born! They are fearfully and wonderfully made!

Doctor Thomas R. Verny— a psychiatrist, writer, academic, and founder of the Pre- and Perinatal Psychology Association of North America-- did research on the life of the unborn child. One of his books, *The Secret Life of the Unborn Child* has become an international bestseller published in 27 countries and has changed the pregnancy and childbirth experience for millions of mothers and fathers. He sees birth as a celebration of life and hope— a symbol of awakening, emerging, changing, and new beginnings. Most people see birth as a physical event, but he says, few see it as a psychological and spiritual event.

There are many influences that can influence the fetus. Verny & Kelly say in their book, *The Secret of the Unborn Child,* "The fetus can see, hear, experience, taste, and on a primitive level, even learn in utero (in the uterus) before birth. Most importantly, the fetus can feel— not with an adult's sophistication but feel nonetheless." We see that the unborn child is an aware, reacting human being who, from the sixth month on, also leads an active emotional life. Because his senses develop and he can hear, see, and experience on a primitive level, and what happens to him during the nine months between conception and birth molds and shapes his personality, says Verny. Even the mother's feelings, especially her deep and persistent patterns of feelings, can have an influence on him. Research shows how the father feels about his wife and unborn child is also an important factor in determining how his child will develop, what his child's personality and characteristics will be, and much more.

If the mother provides her newborn baby with a warm, reassuring, and an inviting environment, it makes a difference because the child is very much aware of how he is born. He can sense gentleness, softness, and a caring touch. He responds positively to a loving and caring environment.

Verny goes on to say that the unborn child's mind is conscious and aware but is not as deeply complex as an adult's mind. He is not capable of understanding the shades of meaning that an adult can put into a simple word or gesture, but he is sensitive to remarkably subtle to emotional nuances. Verny & Weintraub expressed in their book, *Pre-Parenting: Nurturing Your child from Conception* that, "There is no doubt in my mind that at six months after conception the unborn child is a sensing, feeling, aware, and remembering human being." He also says, **"A child conceived in love and cared for lovingly in the womb will benefit throughout life."**

17.1   The link between mother and unborn child

Rosalie Denenfeld studied the link between mothers and their unborn children. She did her Master's Degree on first-time mothers and their unborn children. She focused in her study on these pregnant women's deep levels of awareness within their bodies. These women had to keep a journal of their experiences. They were well educated, of middle-class and married, and had a minimal amount of family and social conflicts. In her studies, she discovered that pregnancy can be the ultimate intimacy possible between human beings. This awakened love within them, made them aware of this intimate love. If mothers can be made aware of this intimate love, it can influence other mothers to bring more love into the world.

Some of the women found their bodies picking up their unborn babies' feelings. One woman explained, "Every once in a while, I have a feeling, but I don't know where it comes from. Then, I realize that I am not the one having the feeling." This mother experienced it during a thunderstorm, with lots of thunder and lightning. She loved storms, to hear the thunder and to see the lightning. One night during a storm, she woke up and was afraid. She got out of bed and walked around in the house. She could not figure it out— then suddenly, she realized that it was not she who is afraid, but it was her unborn baby. She touched him lovingly, talked to him and told him that, although there is a lot of noise, it is quite safe in here. Thereafter, the fear went away, she said.

Denenfeld's main conclusions were that women need to believe they can communicate with and positively influence their unborn babies. There are many interesting ways to stimulate and love your unborn child.

Please take note that there are windows of opportunity during which a child learns certain skills quickly and easily. If this window has pasted it takes much more work and time to learn a skill, and some skills can never be learned again. The period when the brain learns best to make connections is the period between birth and three years of age. During the first their years 70 – 80% of the brain develops.

A small child learns basic trust during his first year of life. If you listen and respond lovingly to your child when he cries, you develop trust in your child. When he cries and you feed, or make him comfortable, or change his diaper, or just hold him lovingly you strengthen his trust in you, and every time you attend to him, he learns that he can trust you. He also learns that he has the ability to "call" you. He then develops trust in himself and later in the world around him.

As children develop, they grow and learn skills. Let us briefly focus on how children develop morally.

CHAPTER 3

HOW CHILDREN DEVELOP MORALLY

Swiss psychologist Jean Piaget (1896-1980) examined moral development the way that children think about right and wrong, rather than whether they acted in a manner that was considered right or wrong.

Piaget described two main stages of moral reasoning in children. He proposed that between the ages of 5-9 years old, children develop moral realism; that is, they believe that morality is conducted by authority figures and breaking rules will lead to punishment. Thus, children tend to judge right and wrong based on the actions of others and the trouble caused by their consequences, rather than the intention behind somebody's actions.

Alternatively, when children reach the age of 9-10 years old, they enter a stage called moral relativism; that is, children realize that morality is subjective to a situation and learn the ability to see a situation from another's perspective. At this stage, children recognize that the intentions behind actions, in addition to the consequence of an action, matter for understanding what is right and wrong.

Piaget essentially theorized that children go from recognizing right and wrong as an absolute, external force, to an internal reasoning that depends on circumstances.

Lawrence Kohlberg (1927-1987) was a moral philosopher and a student of child development. He was the director of Harvard's Center for Moral Education. His area of interest was how children develop a sense of right, wrong, and justice. He observed how growing children advance through definite stages of moral development. His observations and testing of children and adults led him to theorize that humans progress consecutively from one stage to the next, and do not skip any stage or go back to any previous stage. These are stages of thought processing, different modes of thinking and of problem-solving.

Kohlberg, expanded on Piaget's theory by theorizing that there were three levels of moral reasoning. Like Piaget's moral realism stage, Kohlberg believed that in the first level of moral understanding (which he called the preconventional level), morality comes from the outside. Children believe that the consequence of an action dictates the morality of it and this stage lasts till around 9 years old.

Kohlberg discovered that between one and two years of age, children begin to understand there are rules, but usually only follow them if an adult is watching. After two years, they start obeying rules inconsistently, even if an adult is not present. From there they progress further. It is said that all children are born with the capacity to act morally. However, that ability can be lost. Children who are abused or neglected often fail to acquire a basic sense of trust and belonging, and that has an influence on their behavior when they are older.

The second level of morality emerges in most adolescents and adults and is called conventional morality. At this level, people have an internalized sense of right and wrong, but it is still dictated by social rules and authority is not questioned.

Kohlberg believes this last, and third level of morality is not achieved by everybody; in fact, he theorized that only 10-15% actually achieve this stage of moral understanding. In this stage people make up their own moral code based on universal ethical principles; these concepts are often abstract.   Interestingly, Kohlberg's theory highlights the importance of childhood in moral reasoning because he thought that to move up the stages of moral development, you must properly conquer one stage at a time. This means that children would have to master the preconventional stage to move on.

The Bible gives us guidance on how to raise a moral child in Deuteronomy 6:5-9: "Never forget these commands that I am giving you today. Teach them to your children. Repeat them when you are at home and when you are away, when you are resting and when you are working. Tie them on your arms and wear them on your foreheads as a reminder. Write them on the doorpost of your houses and on your gates." You need to teach and guide your children and constantly remind them wherever you go of the commands the Lord has given you.

Effective discipline does not only involve preventing bad behavior or encouraging good conduct. It also includes teaching skills. Nurture the connections in your children's brains that can help them to make better decisions and handle themselves well. Help your children to regulate their emotions, control their impulses, consider other people's feelings, think about consequences, and make thoughtful decisions. Discipline should be respectful and nurturing. Be clear and consistent about your boundaries and guide them with lots of love and care. Connect with them and try to see the world from their view.

Continually connect with your children before redirecting respectfully and compassionately. When you connect and redirect, they will become more receptive rather than reactive. You will build connections in their brain, and these connections will guide them on how to control themselves, as well as to think how others feel and perceive. Help them to regulate their emotions, and to make prudent choices. Instead of telling them what to do, give them experience and strengthen their skills relating to empathy, insight, and morality. They will be happier, do better in school, get into trouble less, and enjoy meaningful relationships.

Proverbs 29:17 says, "Discipline your son and life will be peaceful; he will be a delight to have around." It is our privilege to discipline (teach and guide) our children. It is imperative to understand what discipline is, before applying it to our children. The word **disciplin**_e_ may have different meanings for different people. Let us carefully examine what the word discipline really means.

CHAPTER 4

THE MEANING OF DISCIPLINE

Think of *discipline* as one of the most loving and nurturing actions you can do for your children. Proverbs 13:24 says, "If you don't discipline your son, it shows you don't love him. If you love your child, you will carefully correct him." It says, carefully correct him, there is healing power in love!

Discipline comes from the Latin verb 'discere,' which means *to learn*. It is also derived from another Latin word, 'disciplina,' which was used as far back as the 11th century and means *teaching, learning, and giving instruction*. Discipline means *to teach*! It also comes from the word 'discipulus' or disciple, which means a follower of truth, or respected leader. Children often make their parents or teachers their role models and follow in their footsteps. Thus, it is important to always display positive behavior!

The overall goal of discipline is to teach and to impart knowledge and skills. However, it is mistakenly often equated with punishment and control. The root of the word discipline means *student, pupil,* or *learner*. A disciple, the person receiving discipline, is not a prisoner or recipient of punishment, but one who learns through instruction. Punishment may shut down bad behavior in the short term— but teaching offers skills that last a lifetime! Education comes from the Latin root "educar," which means *to draw forth*. Questions draw forth information— lectures stuff in!

Children need to learn skills that include inhibiting impulses, managing immense angry feelings, and considering the impact of their behavior on others. By lovingly guiding them, you give your children skills; not only to them, but also to your family and the rest of the world! Consider the generational impact this can have as they grow up with these gifts and abilities and raise their own children, who can then pass them on to future generations!

This all begins with rethinking what discipline means, reclaiming that it is not punishment or control, but teaching, building skills, and doing it with love, respect, and an emotional connection. Keep in mind that every child is unique, and no approach will work every time for each child. Try different approaches and get to know your child; discover which approach works best for each individual child.

Discipline is positive; it is teaching, guiding, and learning! Some parents and teachers regard discipline as a precondition for learning. They are of the view that there must be discipline before learning can occur. Kevin Walsh in *Discipline for Character Development* stated that discipline is *how* a person learns— it is purposeful learning!

Discipline is an ongoing process of positive instruction and guidance. Effective discipline is dependent on the relationship you have with your child. This instruction is an investment you make for your children's future, by taking the time to teach your children how to act and respond responsibly, be self-sufficient, and develop competence. Discipline is an act of love! Positive responses from parents can do so much more to nurture positive behavior than negative reactions. Parents need healthy authority that their children can respect.

Authority is the foundation on which your discipline depends. Your children's respect for your authority must be based on love. They will gladly do what you want them to do because they value you and your relationship with them. However, if it is fear-based authority, it can be costly to your relationship. They will learn distance, distrust, deception, all of which result in their staying out of your way. This is not what you want. Therefore, you need to have "a loving" authority and self-control when you guide and teach your children.

Revelation 3:19a says, "Those I love, I correct and discipline . . ." and Proverbs 19:18 says, "Discipline your children while they are young; otherwise, you're just helping them destroy themselves." Discipline is guiding children towards God— to love Him and obey His commandments from the heart.

The purpose of discipline is to teach children skills to make healthy choices and to do what is right because they want to, not because they fear punishment. Effective discipline is moderate, neither very permissive nor very strict. The style of discipline you use in your home will influence the adults your children will become!

Discipline is carried out from love and nurturing. It is something that is done with balance and fairness. It should be different for each child as we are all different, but it should be fair. Each child has a different personality, a different love language, and character. Tailor your discipline to suit each child accordingly.

Children need to be respectful and obedient. Show and model what it is like to be a Christian and love the Lord. It requires an emotional investment on your part. When they act selfishly, you know the heartache that it will bring them. You need to be consistent and fair. We do not live in a perfect world, and we all make mistakes, but we can learn from our mistakes! Be compassionate but firm, and always discipline in love.

Discipline produces character and improves mental and moral development. It can change or form positive behavior where all will benefit from. It can empower children to control their own lives. If there is greatness—discipline is the key to achieving this greatness! Some often think of greatness. The disciples once asked Jesus what determines a person's greatness in the Kingdom of Heaven. Jesus then took a little child in His arms and said to them, "Unless you change and become as trusting and harmless as this little child, you cannot even be admitted into God's Kingdom, much less be considered great. Such innocence comes to adults only by choice. The person who humbles himself like a child is great in the sight of Heaven. (Matt 18:1-4).

Some people punish their children when they are not following rules. They get quick results, but their relationship suffers—because there is a big difference between disciplining in love, and punishing your children by making them suffer pain.

CHAPTER 5

DISCIPLINE AND PUNISHMENT

Discipline is not the same as punishment. Discipline teaches and guides children to learn from their mistakes, rather than making them suffer for them. Teaching and guiding your children are important, but it takes time and energy. When you discipline your children, you want to create acceptable and appropriate behavior and help them to become emotionally mature adults. When you discipline your children, you need to connect with them and demonstrate your love, trust, respect, and understanding to them.

Respect and trust are the foundations of discipline. Children must respect their parents' authority as well as the rights of others. When your discipline is inconsistent or you use harsh, humiliating, and abusive language, your children will disrespect you, and they will lose their trust in you. Effective discipline applied with mutual respect in a firm, fair, reasonable, and consistent way will earn respect and trust. Consistency is very important when you discipline your children. Inconsistency confuses any child, irrespective of their age.

Punishment is so different from discipline. Physical punishment does not facilitate learning. It shifts the focus from the lesson to be learned to who is in control. Punishment shows that the parent is in control, rather than the children learning to control their own behavior. It is negative and causes many other problems. Let us briefly study the effects of physical punishment.

5.1   The effects of physical punishment

Punishment teaches the importance of not getting caught! Punishment's goal is to make the rule violator pay for misconduct. Spanking gets your children to behave quickly, but current research (Ph.D. student Jorge Cuartas testified before the Colombian

Congress in October 2019) has revealed it can do more harm than good. Parents might have been spanked themselves when they were children, so they continue the tradition, but it can cause a long-lasting mark that parents could prevent.

Both parents are responsible for disciplining. When you decide to punish your children, they must understand WHY they are being punished. It is important that children understand that you will not reject them, but rather, you do not like what they did. Never punish your children when you are angry or frustrated; be sure not to take out your anger on your children. Remember, collective punishment (when you punish all instead of the one who did the offence) is very wrong! Be responsible when you give consequences or punishment.

Evidence shows corporal punishment increases children's behavioral problems over time and has no positive outcomes. Corporal punishment is a violation of children's rights to respect physical integrity and human dignity, health, development, education, and freedom from torture and other cruel, inhumane, or degrading treatment or punishment.

Hitting children does not teach them about responsibility, conscience development, or self-control. "Hitting children does not teach them right from wrong," says Elizabeth Gershoff, PhD, an expert on the effects of corporal punishment on children. "Spanking gets their attention, but they have not internalized why they should do the right thing in the future. They may behave when the adult is there but do whatever they want at other times."

Spanking children does not facilitate learning. It may teach children what not to do, but it fails to teach children what is expected of them and what the alternate behavior should be. In addition, physical discipline is most often used when the parent is frustrated or without any other resources.

5.2 Negative effects of physical punishment revealed by research (end violence against children on the web) include:

* The more a child is spanked, the lower his IQ becomes compared to others; the difference can be as great as 5%.
* Spanking may cause a child's mental abilities to slow down.
* There is a link between spanking and a child's aggressive behavior.
* Spanking is a traumatic experience. Traumatic stress affects the brain adversely.
* Hitting is associated with fear and stress; they usually have a harder time focusing on learning.
* Spanking does not foster independent thinking.
* It increases anxiety and fear.
* It thwarts the development of empathy and compassion for others.
* It makes children angry and heightens aggression toward others.
* It decreases compliance and increases resistance.
* It harms your relationship with your children and decreases their self-esteem.
* It can potentially cause unintended and severe physical and/or emotional injury.
* It increases an array of undesirable social and psychological behaviors.
* It can teach that violence is an acceptable way to handle conflict.

5.3 American Humane Association encourages parents to use positive and appropriate discipline:

* Always discipline with love and listen and communicate with your child.

* Focus on the behavior and not on the child.
* Respond immediately and relate the duration and severity of the discipline to the offending behavior.
* Be realistic, calm, fair, and never harm or injure the child.
* Set clear boundaries and make it a learning opportunity.
* Remember to be consistent, creative, and develop rules and expectations in advance.
* Model, reward or praise desirable behaviors and encourage the child's cooperation.
* Provide a warm and caring home and respect your child's viewpoint.

Spanking is less effective in changing behavior in the long-term and is associated with negative outcomes in many areas. However, there are many non-spanking discipline approaches that can be just as damaging as spanking. Isolating children for long periods of time, humiliating them, terrifying them by screaming threats, and using other forms of verbal or psychological aggression are a few examples. These disciplinary practices wound children's minds even when their parents never physically touch them.

Holmes and Robbins (1987) found that unfair, inconsistent, and harsh discipline by parents predicted later alcohol and depressive disorders. ("Discipline with Dignity" in the *Journal of Child Psychology and Psychiatry and Allied Discipline* 28:399-415))

5.4   Effects of physical punishment and the brain

Spanking and inflicting pain create fear and terror and are counterproductive. Instead of children becoming aware and recognizing what they did wrong, they will tend to focus on your response, and how unfair, mean and scary you are. This undermines the primary goal of discipline, which is to change behavior and build the brain. Spanking is negative when you want to build respectful relationships with your children. Teach them the lessons you want them to learn and encourage optimal development.

Siegel and Bryson, in their book *No-Drama Discipline*, stated that children have the right to be free from any form of violence, especially at the hand of the people they trust the most to protect them. When parents spank, something happens to the child physiologically and neurologically. The brain understands pain as a threat. The child experiences a biological paradox. They are born with an instinct to go to their parents for protection when they are hurt or afraid, but, when the parents are the source of their child's pain and fear, it can be very confusing for the child's brain. The brain can become disorganized; this is referred to as disorganized attachment. When this happens, cortisol, which is toxic to the brain, is released. Repeated experiences of rage and terror can result in negative impacts and can have long-lasting effects on the brain's development. Harsh and severe punishment can change the brain, and connections and brain cells die.

Janusz Korczak states: "There are many terrible things in this world. But the worst is when a child is afraid of his father, mother, or teacher. He fears them, instead of loving and trusting them."

Spanking can teach a child that the parent has no effective strategy other than inflicting pain. Do you want your child to learn that this is the way to resolve a conflict, particularly with someone who is defenseless and cannot fight back? Humans' brains are wired to avoid pain. The part of the brain that mediates physical pain also processes social rejection. Children do whatever it takes to avoid pain and social rejection. Consequently, your children will not be open to learning, but may start lying and hiding, and not communicating openly with you.

You can appeal to part of the brain with loving guidance and teaching. When you discipline, make use of your children's higher thinking brain, rather than their lower reptilian brain. When you cause your children to experience fear, pain, and anger, you activate the primitive, reactive brain, instead of directing it to the receptive, thinking, and potentially intelligent region of the brain; the latter helps children to make healthy choices. When you activate the reactive part of the brain, you miss the opportunity of developing the thinking part of the brain.

Punishment has different impacts on different children. Lawrence Cohen in *Playful Parenting* states, "... Punishment has the least impact on the very children who are most likely to be punished." Certain children are more impulsive and find it more difficult to develop a conscience. Certain traits make children more susceptible to getting into trouble. In addition, these very traits make them less able to make changes to their behavior because of punishment or the fear of it.

Children who misbehave need help in organizing themselves, not punishment. Cohen asserted that most punishment disorganizes children. They need to process incoming information and organize an effective response. To organize themselves, they need a quiet space with toys, blankets, and pillows. You can rock them in a rocking chair, go to the swings, hug them, and hold them close.

This is more effective for younger children, but older children can sometimes benefit from this, too. Cohen adds that disorganized behavior is partly the result of not getting enough of those kinds of comforts or rhythms in their life when they were infants and toddlers. He states that older children need a structured schedule— for example, art projects and safe roughhousing to foster this type of cognitive organization. Strategies and effective options for disciplining your children can give them practice using the thinking part of their brain. Some strategies can equip them to become responsible beings who do what you expect of them.

Maybe you have heard that time-outs are a very good alternative to physical punishment. You may have used time-outs to discipline your children. Let us briefly review time-outs and the effect it has on children.

5.5   Time-outs

Time-outs are often used with a lot of anger. Furthermore, time-outs impel children to experience isolation and/or rejection, even if they are done in a loving way. Ask yourself when your children make a mistake or misbehave if you want them to repeatedly be isolated and by themselves. Young children experience this as a rejection. Remember brain connections are formed from repeated experiences.

Assist your children to experience positive behavior; instead of a time-out, ask them to practice handling a situation differently. When, for example, their tone of voice or words were disrespectful, ask them to try it again and communicate what they are saying respectfully. When they have been mean to a sibling, you can ask them to do three kind things for their affected sibling before bedtime. In this way, they are afforded opportunities to repeat positive behavior, and it begins to get wired into their brain. Correct negative behavior by suggesting positive action instead of negative experiences.

Empathetic decisions can empower children with good behavior, but time-outs deprive them of it. Why give time-outs? Do you want to calm them and make them reflect on their behavior? Time-outs make children angrier and do not afford them the time to think about what they have done wrong. Rather, they think of how mean you are.

During time-outs, your children need your comfort and calm presence. However, if you force them to go off and sit alone, they may experience rejection. This may give them the message that, when they do not do the right thing, you do not want to be near them.

Rather use time-ins where you sit with your children and help them to reflect on their behavior after you have connected and calmed them down. When you sit with your children, they can talk to you and tell you what they want. When children need to reflect, it should be in a relationship and not in isolation. You can help them to see their own mind and the mind of others and have empathy. Mindsight is insight; thus, empathy and integration are the basis of social and emotional intelligence.

Help your children to self-regulate their emotions; do not punish or make them pay for their mistakes; instead, create a place where they can be calm and think when it is necessary. Together make a space with toys, books, or stuffed animals where they can go and calm themselves down if they choose to do so.

There are many alternatives to punishments that can build your children's brain and enhance your relationship with them. These alternatives should be linked to their behavior, shape their brain, and strengthen the relationship between you and your children. Model calmness and self-control to your children.

Physical punishment can have a negative effect on self-concept. Let us briefly scrutinize what effect physical punishment has on a child's self-concept and self-esteem.

5.6   Self-concept and punishment

A self-concept is the image you construct of who you are and how you fit into the world. It is maintained, protected, and enhanced by the way you interpret events, by the choices you make, and by your internal dialogue. You need to tell your children they are able, valuable, and responsible individuals. You need to remind them that you love them and that you care about them.

Often negative self-esteem hides behind labels such as unmotivated, undisciplined, unable, or uninterested. It was found that people with a negative self-regard tend to be more destructive, more anxious, more stressed, and are more likely to manifest psychosomatic symptoms than people who have an average or high self-regard.

Criticism has a negative effect on your child's self-image. A person's self-concept is mainly determined by how he or she reacts to failures and disappointments. Children can quickly sense whether they are valued and able to do things in and around the house. They are also able to tell whether they are valued by their parents or whether they are just another member of the family.

A negative self-concept makes children feel uncertain about themselves, causes discordant relationships in the family, and makes them afraid to take risks. Parents, help your children to develop a positive self-image!

How does negative discipline influence self-image? Children with a positive self-image will not be influenced negatively when they are justly disciplined. To dehumanize and emphasize their low self-esteem can harm children even more. It is very wrong to discipline with an unsupportive attitude. You can correct behavior when you are calm and do it in love. Punishment is wrong when it is unfair, unearned, undeserved, unmerited, out of context, and/or given for the wrong reasons.

Do not be too rigid or inflexible with your children. They learn more easily when they are encouraged to do the right thing. You need to have a unique relationship with your children. In all relationships, there needs to be mutual respect.

A child needs consistent and responsible discipline. Children learn responsibility when they have opportunities to learn in an atmosphere of kindness, firmness, dignity, and respect. You need to provide these opportunities and create a warm atmosphere in your home. Do not raise your children in an atmosphere of blame, shame, and pain. Always ask yourself if you are empowering or discouraging your children.

5.7   Sad stories

Some of the saddest stories described in Lawrence Cohen's book, *Playful Parenting*, are of parents, mostly men, who criticized and harshly punished their children and loved ones. They battered their wives and girlfriends, many of them hit their children, and almost all of them had been beaten when they were boys.

They passed on the violence that they had endured and some of them even defended it: "My daddy hit me with a belt, and there is nothing wrong with me." Cohen explained when they could break through their defensiveness and really talk about what it was like for them growing up, many of them said that the worst part was not the violence, but the lack of any tenderness from anybody.

Cohen found that these men were not terribly loveable but was unsure whether they had once been regular little babies. When they started heading down the wrong path, not one of them got any love or gentle guidance, only harsh discipline. Parents are often reluctant to give out love to people who have behaved badly, even when it is what they need. When people are at their worst, they need love the most!

Continued threats have no meaning, and continuous reprimanding is not disciplining. Be consistent when you discipline. Never discipline or punish with sarcasm or disrespect. Have a healthy attitude toward discipline, and when you punish, punish with one hand and comfort with the other one.

Discipline also involves teaching our children to control their big emotions which is not always easy for them to do, let us look at self-control and how we can guide our children to grow more control of their emotions.

CHAPTER 6

SELF-CONTROL AND RESILIENCE

"In childhood and youth, the character is most impressible. The power of self-control should then be acquired. By the fireside and at the family board influences are exerted, whose results are as enduring as eternity. More than any natural endowment, the habits established in early years decide whether a man will be victorious or vanquished in the battle of life. Youth is the sowing time. It determines the character of the harvest, for this life and for the life to come." (DA 101)

Self-control is the ability to control our behavior. It is the skill to delay gratification and resist unwanted behaviors. It prevents us from screaming at others when we are angry or from punching someone when they do us wrong. It also stops us from crying uncontrollably when we do not get our way.

Self-control seems to come naturally to some people, while others struggle with it. It is a character trait that is very valuable in life. Self-control can assist children to develop intellectually, socially, emotionally, and spiritually. It can even develop respect for themselves. Children are never too young to learn self-control. If you wait until they are older to teach it, you may miss the window of opportunity for it. It will also be more difficult to teach or learn it later. Proverbs 22:6 says: "Start a child on the right path while he's young, and when he is old, he will not forget what he's been taught."

Self-control is part of learning about obedience; this is one of the indispensable childhood spiritual lessons that will lay a foundation for a lifelong relationship with God and with man. How can children be obedient to God if they are unable to be obedient to their earthly parents? Self-control is one of the lessons that you need to teach your children when they are still very young. Guide them lovingly and help them to control their emotions, but more importantly— you need to have self-control yourself, and model it to them!

To teach self-control requires not only a great deal of patience but also persistence and consistency in your approach. It is a skill that enables children and adults to practice restraint by managing their thoughts, emotions, feelings, and behaviors and not acting on their impulses. They need to learn to wait their turn in line, to sit still in a venue when a performance is going on, and not to throw a tantrum when they do not get what they desire.

Children have limited self-control since that part of their brain which is responsible for emotional control is still underdeveloped. Over time, developing self-control helps children to make friends, build relationships, and find their way through life.

6.1   How to teach your children self-control

It is a difficult task for little ones to remain in control of themselves. We as parents need to give them skills that help them to make good decisions when they are upset. Teach them to take deep breaths or count to ten. You can also teach them what is happening in their brains when they feel they are losing control and how to avoid it.

Even small children have the capacity to stop and think instead of hurting someone with their words or their fists. They will not always make the best decisions, but the more they practice alternatives other than lashing out, the stronger and more capable their brains will become.

By teaching your children self-control or self-discipline, responsibility, cooperation, and problem-solving skills help them establish an excellent foundation, earning dignity and respect. When they have mastered these characteristics and skills, they will feel a greater sense of belonging and significance, which will manifest itself through positive behavior.

It is important to have rules which children need to follow. It is necessary to establish a daily routine, and have regular times for eating, sleeping, playing, and working. Establish a consistent, predictable time to do certain activities. This patterning creates a secure environment for children and helps them to feel safe. It also helps them to know what is going to happen next. Do not give your children too much, too soon, or too easily. Make sure that you are there for them when they need you and guide them lovingly and gently in what they need to do.

Children need limits so that they don't feel out of control, and they respond more positively when parents stand by those limits. They keep testing the limits to see if their parents will uphold them. When you insist on obedience and help children to get control of themselves, it can help them develop inner controls.

Assist children to change the way they think about a situation. Prepare them mentally for difficult or different situations than they are used to. Repeating instructions or giving them gentle and timely reminders before they face a difficult situation is a positive way to prepare them mentally. Or you could ask them for a solution by asking them how they would solve the problem. This can help them to think and enable them to come up with creative solutions. Teach them to take deep breaths and inhale slowly in and out. This can help in more than one situation.

Model positive behavior and your children will learn how you handle difficult situations. Then, when they feel angry or frustrated, they will remember how you handled it. Give children a reward when they show self-control. Instill trust in them and let them know that you are always there for them when they want to discuss a problem. Teach them to think about why they are angry before responding to any situation and compliment them when they practice restraint.

There is no specific age to depict when self-control is fully developed. It varies according to individual children and their nature. Teach them words that can help them express their feelings and emotions thereby they can also develop self-control.

You are role models for your children. They identify with you, and you transmit norms and values to them while you generate a warm, loving, and happy atmosphere in your home. Remember, education is only possible if two people have a relationship with each other, and the nature and success of education depends on the quality of this relationship! By being a role model, you can help your children to develop appropriate behavior, self-control, responsibility, and accountability; this will also increase their self-esteem.

The way you use control, and how you support your children are two main aspects of parent-child relationships. This will lead to the success or failure of the relationship and, subsequently, the child's upbringing. This will also affect how well children accept your values and live by them. How much control you use and how much support you provide will determine what type of parenting style you use.

We all tend to parent the way we were raised, but you can make an intentional effort to change your approach. Let us briefly examine four different styles of discipline and what the possible outcome of each of these educational styles has on children. Furthermore, we will briefly explore what possible outcome each style will have on your children's spiritual development. The four styles we will briefly explore are the authoritarian approach, the neglectful approach, the permissive approach, and the authoritative approach.

Resilience is the ability to become strong, healthy, and successful after something dreadful has happened. We all have painful experiences. Resilience is the ability to bounce back or try again. It is an important aspect of emotional and mental health. As much as we want to protect our children from difficulties in life. From experiencing crisis, change, or loss we cannot! However, we can give them tools to be resilient.

Life is not about what happens to us but what we do about it, or how we respond to it. Resilience can be learned and developed. It is part of our emotional intelligence. When we face a problem and we have learned resilience, we can focus on finding a solution rather than getting depressed and feeling like a victim. It is emotional strength!

You can develop resilience in your children by telling them stories from their childhood; about the things they did when they were small. This will reinforce the connection between you and your children, especially when they love hearing these stories. Relate, "On the day you were born... When you used to sleep at Grandma's house when Mommy had to work at night..." or "I remember the time when we took you to the park and..." All these reinforce connections for your children. These stories encourage the development of coping skills and resilience, even when children experience disruptive or traumatic events. Stories also anchor children in ways that make the stress of outside events more manageable. You can provide a foundation of resilience through a strong sense of self and family— stories very powerfully can do that.

Teach your children to be flexible. Flexible children adjust well to different ideas and changing situations. Teach them to try different kinds of food, listen to different kinds of music, read different kinds of books, and expose them to different cultures, different social groups, and different hobbies.

Teach your children responsibility. When they feel bad about something, ask them, "What can you do to feel better about it?" or "What can you learn from this?"

From two years old, you can increase their emotional vocabulary. Teach them to say, "I like this..." or "I am not happy with..." "I want to do this..." "I prefer this or that..." "I will be happy if I can..." "If I can go..." or "I am upset..." or "I was sad..."

Try to focus on the good in every situation. Make a habit of seeing the good in everything. This will help them respond better to loss, change, major illnesses, or any other challenge.

Assist your children to master a skill. This can build their confidence. Help them to move and improve that skill, even if they have difficulties.

Expose your children to others or to stories of people who have overcome great difficulties and were successful in the end. Tell them they always have a choice about what to do.

Teach your children gratitude and to be positive. Assist them to have a purpose in life and something to look forward to. Help them to give their time for the greater good of society. Let them volunteer their time, skills, and money to what they consider a good cause and use the good feeling as their reward.

The Serenity Prayer is a positive concept to know in time of a challenge: "God, grant me the courage to change the things I can, Serenity to accept the things I cannot change, and the Wisdom to know the difference!"

CHAPTER 7

DIFFERENT STYLES OF DISCIPLINE

There are many different styles or approaches to discipline. The reasons for these differences include culture, personality, family size, parental background, socio-economic status, educational level, and religion or beliefs. It is essential that parents cooperate with each other as they combine their unique styles.

Parents are the major influence in their children's lives. Their perception of how children should be raised is crucial in determining their children's behavior. Researchers have found that other factors such as genes, peers, culture, gender, and financial status are of lesser importance.

Studies have revealed a correlation between parenting styles and school competence, such as delinquency, violence, sexual activity, antisocial behavior, alcohol and substance abuse, depression, anxiety, and self-perception.

Power and authority are concepts often used in today's world. People have power over others if they are taller, stronger, and more superior to others. Authority, however, cannot be forced on people. You earn it by the way you act in everyday life. You receive it because people look up to you.

Diana Baumrind, a clinical and developmental psychologist (from Cowell Memorial Hospital in Berkley), studied parenting styles and concluded that they mainly differ in four important areas: parents' warmth and nurturance; discipline strategy; communication skills; and expressions of maturity. She postulated three types of parenting styles: authoritarian, permissive, and authoritative.

There are also other styles and combinations of styles that parents use to discipline their children; however, to provide clarity, some distinct styles are briefly discussed. It is not about how you act once or twice, but the pattern in how you raise your children and act most of the time. Let us briefly examine four styles and how they influence children as they become adults.

7.1 The authoritarian approach

The authoritarian style has been referred to as the iron rod; it is dictatorial and harsh. Children are to be seen and not heard. Communication is strictly one way; parent to child, usually in loud-voiced commands, but child-to-parent communication is poor. The children are expected to obey without questioning. There is not much warmth and nurturance, but strict discipline and high expectations. These parents show their children little affection; however, obedience, respect, and tradition are highly valued by the parents. Rules are not to be questioned, and the parents are always right. These children obey their parents to avoid punishment and become passive. Authoritarian parents use power to discipline their children. Children are not allowed to express themselves. These parents believe only they know what is good for their children. They give orders continually, without any freedom on the part of the children. They don't allow their children to make choices. They admonish, "Do it because I say so!"

Authoritarian parenting is a restrictive, punitive style in which parents advise their children to follow their directions and respect their work. The parents are seldom flexible about their demands. There is no middle road or compromise, and they do not reach a consensus with their children. These parents are very strict and use excessive control. They also mainly use physical punishment. This almost non-interactive style has serious developmental drawbacks.

7.1.1 Possible outcomes of an authoritarian home:
* These children seldom become entrepreneurs or creative people.

* If they do not break away from this lifestyle, they will treat their spouses and children in the same manner.

* They never learn to reason about a matter, nor do they know how to evaluate or judge situations.

* They are often filled with fear.

* These children rank lower in happiness, social competence, and self-esteem.

* They have not acquired the skills to make meaningful decisions in a complex world.

* They may turn completely against this kind of authority and become rebellious.

* They are indecisive individuals, incapable of dealing with difficult moral decisions.

* They are susceptible to antisocial peer pressure; during adolescence this influence is strong.

* Studies have shown that boys in this category have the highest level of violence.

* Teenagers are less self-reliant, persistent, and socially graceful, and have a lower self-esteem.

* They lack social competence and rarely initiate activities.

* They show less intellectual curiosity, are not spontaneous, and rely on the voice of authority.

7.1.2   Possible influence on their spiritual lives:

* Children from authoritarian homes usually do not have a strong conscience.

* They tend to reject the values of their parents and embrace negative values.

* They usually reject religion.

* If they are religious, they may try to be perfect in every detail of the Christian life, hoping to earn God's favor and avoid His punishment through their efforts of good works.

* Their personalities may lack warmth, compassion, and empathy for the plight of others.

* Their God is a wrathful, vengeance-seeking judge who is ready to destroy if they do not measure up.

* They do not discuss issues with their parents; they reason, "Why bother? I am always wrong or ignored."

* They distance themselves from their parents by rebelling against their values and beliefs.

7.1.3. Story of a person who was raised with this approach

This is the story of Martin Luther. The reformer grew up in a very strict authoritarian home. Eric Erikson in his book, *The Young Man Luther*, described his upbringing. Here is a brief outline of his childhood, his parents, and the kind of educational approach they used.

Martin Luther's father was a tense, ambitious man. He was a farmer and later worked in the mines. He wanted his son, Martin, to do better for himself than he had. He wanted Martin to study law. At that time, this was a highly prestigious profession. Martin's parents were both very strict. They both beat him often and very severely—his mother once caned him until he bled for stealing a nut.

Luther matured late. He had difficulty in coming to terms with himself, his role, and the tasks that he had to do. Luther had no identity. It was Luther's belief that you must punish yourself to be acceptable to God. He had an impulsive and obsessive personality. At times he was desperately anxious, compulsively neurotic, torn by doubts, and even suffered weird attacks and hallucinations. Erikson expressed the view that Luther's greatness lies in the fact that he could discover a cause in his agonizing struggle.

Luther's monastic teachers said, "God does not hate you—you hate Him." Dr. Staupitz was his fatherly sponsor for identity, and he became a positive figure for Luther. Dr. Staupitz was convinced of his student's gifts and allowed Luther to preach and lecture. He refused to argue with Luther but put him to work! Luther started preaching and lecturing; he started to verbalize what was inside of him.

Because Luther was no longer required to keep quiet, words and vocalization became critical for him to discover his identity. His monastic teachers knew that he needed to speak and discover who he was. Because of these changes, Luther could form genuine relationships. He became his true self. Previously, he had no identity because he could not speak and relate to that with which he struggled. He studied and turned to the Bible and came to know the positive God; this helped him to find his identity and place in the world.

Stress, trauma, and/or no basic trust can influence a developmental phase. Certain patterns are formed during the developmental phases of childhood, and these have a determinative impact on later life. This can, in turn, have a radical influence on one's faith and concept of God. Naturally, parents are the main influences in this regard. Erikson stressed that maternal warmth is essential for a sense of identity in adult life. Without basic trust, which is developed during the first year of life, identity is not possible. An unhealthy relationship with your parents is unconsciously projected in your religion.

7.2   The neglectful approach

The name explains it clearly. Some parents tend to ignore their children. Neglectful parenting is also referred to as uninvolved, detached, dismissive, and hands-off. These parents do not show much warmth and have little control; they are generally not involved and remain uninvolved in their children's lives. They show little concern for their children's needs. Sometimes these parents do not want to sacrifice their convenience. They make weak attempts to guide their children with choices or other guidelines for raising responsible people.

Neglectful parents are undemanding, low in responsiveness, they do not set limits, and dismiss their children's emotions and opinions. Some parents can even be abusive to their children, while others physically mistreat their children. Some parents do not supply their children's daily needs such as food, shelter, and clothing. Sometimes they may even be well-educated and career-conscious people. They leave the task of bringing up their children to the nanny, baby-sitter, or the teacher. According to Donna Habernicht, who wrote *How to Help Your Child Really Love Jesus,* sometimes these parents provide well for their children, but they are not emotionally involved.

What results can be expected from parents who remain uninvolved, abusive, mistreat their children, do not provide for their needs, or are not emotionally involved in their lives?

7.2.1 Here are some possible consequences of the neglectful approach:

* These children often react in the same way as children who are from authoritarian homes.
* They often rebel and embrace negative values that they pick up outside of their home.
* They may have emotional problems because of neglect.
* They may become emotionally withdrawn from social situations.
* These children may have disturbed attachment, which also affects relationships later in life.
* In adolescence, they may show patterns of absenteeism from school or work, and delinquency.

* They may be inclined to damage others' property because of the lack of emotional support.

* These children often have an *"I don't care"* attitude because no one has cared for or about them.

* This approach often leads children to become narcissists.

7.2.2   Their spiritual life may be affected as follows:

 * These children usually are not very religious and usually reject their parents' religion.

* They may not have strong values because they have not been taught or disciplined consistently.

* Their God may be perceived as a distant ruler of the universe, uninvolved in His children.

* God may be regarded as someone who does not care what happens to them.

* These children are often rebellious, without respect for God or man's authority.

7.3   The permissive approach

This approach is also referred to as the indulgent, free-range, nondirective, and lenient parenting style. Permissive parents are also labeled as neglectful or disengaged parents. They have poor discipline and hardly any structure, little parent-to-child communication, but a great deal of child-to-parent communication with a few expectations. Some of these parents are nurturing, warm, and accepting. Their main concerns are to allow children to express their creativity or individuality and/or to make them happy in the belief that this will teach them right from wrong. Ironically, these children are the unhappiest of all.

This style was popular in Germany during Hitler's time; children and adults who were raised in a permissive home followed Hitler who demanded unquestioning obedience. These parents conditioned their children for Hitler. (*The Fountain* - Dinwiddie 1995).

This approach is the opposite of the authoritarian approach. Parents apply minimum control or discipline. There are very few demands and hardly any rules. They believe their children are free, should make their own decisions, and do not need any guidance. But how can they if they have not been taught? Perhaps they think their children know how to behave and therefore should also know what is right and what is wrong. In these homes, though, there is freedom without order. There are no specific guidelines on how or what to do in certain situations, not even how to make decisions. The parents say, "You can do anything you want." These children are *lost* in the sense that they are left to their own inadequate devices. These parents are not even involved in or with their children's problems. They do not understand their children or their problems. However, their children do not take them seriously because they (the parents?) do not really care.

When these children grow up, they need guidance, protection, and a framework of rules. It is only when they know what is right and wrong that they will feel safe and secure. Absolute freedom does not exist as one always lives under some kind of authority. Permissiveness is neglecting children to an extreme degree.

7.3.1 Some of the possible outcomes these children may display:

* These children may lack self-confidence and creativity.
* They may exhibit strong aggression and a lack of self-control.
* Later in life, they may constantly be late for work or appointments because they have never had responsibilities, a set routine and/or stability in their upbringing.

* They may have little or no perseverance and feel very insecure.

* They may have the attitude, "This is me and you have to accept me for who I am."

* These children may be susceptible to all kinds of influences inside and outside of their homes.

* They may never learn to make decisions or to evaluate situations in which they had no guidance.

* They may sometimes brag about themselves but become pathetic and very uncertain about themselves when they realize others have seen through them.

* They may not experience much happiness and be able to self-regulate.

* They are likely to exhibit psychological problems such as anxiety and depression.

* They may commit violence and engage in antisocial behavior.

* It is linked with delinquency, substance abuse, and sexual activity.

* Children may learn a false sense of control over adults, which could lead to an increase in manipulative behavior; furthermore, because rules are not firmly in place, they may try to manipulate rules as well as people.

* They may do poorly in school and have higher rates of misbehavior in adult authority.

* They may not have learned to control or discipline themselves and cannot develop self-respect.

* They may try to control their parents and others.

* Their unmet psychological needs are likely to make them vulnerable and easily discouraged.

* Permissive parenting may thwart their social development and positive self-esteem.

* They may have difficulty controlling their impulses.

* They are likely to be immature and reluctant to accept responsibility.
* They may also have sleep disturbances.

7.3.2 The possible ways these children may react toward religion include:

* They may tend to be impulsive.
* They may not grow up with a strong set of values.
* They may be irresponsible and have a weak moral structure.
* They may wait for rewards, which never appeal to them.
* They may not regard sin as a major universal problem.
* They are inclined to believe their God is an accepting and loving God who smiles and looks the   other way when they misbehave.

The authoritarian, neglecting, and permissive parenting styles appear to be clustered at one end of the parenting spectrum; none of the styles have been linked to positive outcomes, presumably because they minimize opportunities for children to learn to cope with their stresses.

Too much control and too many demands may limit children's opportunities to make decisions for themselves, or to make their needs known to their parents. On the other hand, children in permissive households may lack the direction and guidance necessary to develop appropriate morals and goals.

7.4   The authoritative approach

The authoritative approach is sometimes also called the communicative or democratic approach. These parents have a great deal of warmth, good communication, and moderate and realistic expectations. Their discipline is moderate. They are nurturing, create a loving home environment, and provide a high degree of emotional support. They are firm, fair, and respectful in their dealings with their children.

These parents realize their children need guidance in an atmosphere of warmth, love, and flexibility. They know that children need to understand why some things are right and others are wrong. Children need to be taught to reason and to know how to make decisions. These parents are polite, honest, and trustworthy, and are role models to their children. Children need freedom with order as well as limited choices, which these parents realize. They usually say, "You may choose within these limits." The latter shows respect for all.

These parents want their children to become responsible adults, are consistent, and have empathy for and understand their children. They are there for their children, to guide and show them the way. These parents can forgive because they know how easy it is to fall by the way. They understand the love of Jesus; therefore, they can be true examples for their children. Authoritative parents can understand their children's feelings and teach them how to regulate them. They help them to find appropriate outlets to solve problems. These parents encourage independence, but they still place limits and controls on their children's actions, and verbal give-and-take is allowed.

In the authoritative home, children are given alternatives, and are encouraged to make decisions and accept responsibility for their actions and decisions; this leads to self-empowerment. The children's opinions are valued and respected; thus, all parties benefit. The parents use reason, negotiation, and persuasion; they do not use force to gain their children's cooperation. They also set appropriate limits and standards for behavior. This style is characterized by mutual understanding and is based on mutual benefit. The parents also provide a balance between control and independence. They encourage academic success and the children's grades reflect that. Parents are involved with their children. Authoritative parenting helps build a close parent-child connection and relationships. They first connect to, and then redirect.

Parent-child connectedness is an emotional bond between parent and child. This parent-child connectedness involves a protective factor in the prevention of problems such as drug abuse, violence, unintended pregnancy, and school failure. Talking with children about thoughts and feelings strengthens relationships and helps children to develop mindsight.

7.4.1 The possible consequences of the authoritative approach include:

* These children usually display responsibility, patience, and lots of self-confidence.

* They are content with their life situations and work.

* They can cooperate well with other people and can control their emotions.

* They usually become leaders and organizers in society.

* Both parents and children make rules for their mutual benefit.

* These children are happy, capable, and successful in what they do most of the time.

* They usually are confident and competent.

* They are likely to develop high self-esteem, a positive self-concept, and great self-worth.

* They are less rebellious and generally, more successful in life.

* They are usually well-adjusted.

* They generally have immense self-respect, and respect for authority.

* They are usually accountable and can control their impulses.

* They are less likely to use or abuse drugs or alcohol and be involved in delinquency.

* They usually report less anxiety and depression and show the least amount of violence.

* With connectedness, the parents help their infants learn the important developmental skill of self-   regulation   of emotions and socialization; furthermore, their distress is soothed, needs are met,   and alertness enhanced.

* They usually have a sense of mastery and competence, an internal working model of how   relationships with others work and thus, are able to shape future relationships with peers and   eventually with romantic partners.

7.4.2 The possible consequences of this approach on children's spiritual life are as follows:

* Children raised with this approach usually have strong values and are willing to stand up for them.

* They are likely to be helpful and caring toward others.

* They usually have the strength to resist peer pressure.

* They are likely to know what is right and have a strong conscience that guides their actions.

* They are likely to have a strong moral character.

* They are generally positive about the values and religion they have learned from their parents.

* They generally believe their God is loving, caring, and forgives their misdeeds, they grow in faith and grace.

* They also generally believe their God is the perfect blend of mercy and justice— a God who draws   them   closer   to Himself.

* They usually show a greater interest in their parents' faith in God.

* The connected approach allows the mother to respond with sensitivity and consistency to her child's needs,   and she sends a series of important messages to her infant that builds trust and security.

Research has proven repeatedly that parenting styles have a direct correlation with how children will grow up, how they live and whether they will abide by the rules in society. A study, known as the "*Value Genesis Study*," was conducted in 1989 by a Department of Education in the United States. This study involved approximately 11,000 young people between the ages of 12 and 18. Researchers found that the youth who had a growing, mature Christian faith and healthy morals, consistently came from homes where the parents were not only loving and caring, and involved in their children's lives, but also enforced healthy standards of behavior in their homes.

We all tend to parent in the same way we were raised, but one can change! You may not even question your parenting style until you start having problems with your children. It may seem as though suddenly and unexpectedly your current parenting style is not working anymore, and you do not know why. Good parenting does not necessarily come naturally and easily, but there are skills you can learn to meet the challenge of good parenting. Find a sound, practical parenting style and master it. An authoritative style is well worth the effort. Parents' instructions should be constant and consistent. Religious instruction must be by word and example all the time. Remember to train a child in the way he should go, and when he is old, he will not depart from it. Even if children do depart for a time, they will, in all likelihood return.

7.5 What should you expect from a positive, respectful parenting style?

* Eliminating the need for spanking, time-outs, and grounding.

* Move from reward and punishment to influencing and guiding good behavior.

* Learn effective techniques that make *temper tantrums* a thing of the past.

* A parenting style that is easy to implement and produces effective results.

* A parenting style that is effective throughout all the stages of childhood.

* Guiding children to be cooperative, responsible, and happy.

* The ability to create a positive and loving relationship with your children.

* The ability to raise children who will be responsible adults who are able to cope in the world.

Another approach is *the connecting approach*. It is important for these parents to connect with their children. They use an empathetic approach and have a close relationship with them. It is vital for their children to have empathy and be emotionally resilient. They connect emotionally, listen to their children, and value their brain development. This approach fits in beautifully with the authoritative style.

Donna Habernicht describes two different families, which may help you to better understand the above parenting styles:

"The evening meal was the most important meal in Maria and Jorge's home— the only time they ate together as a family. Nothing was allowed to interfere with this cherished family time. Their kids, ages 4 to 13, eagerly anticipated this special time with their father. They knew he was very busy ministering to the people in the church and community, but, at this special time of the day, Dad was theirs— no interruptions allowed.

Sometimes Dad even got home a little early, and they could play a quick game of catch or look at an interesting new website together before eating. Occasionally, a serious emergency came up and Dad did not make it home for the evening meal, but the kids understood. Their father, the minister, had to respond to emergencies or be out of town sometimes on important business.

After mealtime, the family worshiped God before going about their evening activities. Jorge generally visited church families, studied the Bible with interested families, or attended committee meetings. Maria helped the children with their homework assignments and tucked the younger ones into bed. Jorge tried to get home by 9:30, in time to have a quiet conversation with the older children and then with Maria after all the children were in bed.

Things were different in Elena and Eduardo's home. Elena served the evening meal, but she and the children generally ate alone. Usually, Eduardo felt he was too busy to come home to eat, so, most evenings, he grabbed fast food and continued working until long after the children had gone to sleep. When he did make it home for the evening meal, he answered his cell phone repeatedly and often ate hurriedly, running out the door for every 'emergency.' Rarely was there time to play ball with the children or hear about their day. Generally, Elena had worship with the children without him. Eduardo's children barely knew him.

Elena yearned for support with the child-rearing, but Eduardo thought he was too busy to be involved. Most of the time, she had to deal with school assignments, misbehavior, family worship, and an endless list of daily decisions, alone. Sometimes Eduardo would get involved if there was a serious discipline problem. He was very strict, not inclined to listen to the child's point of view and favored severe punishment.

Fast-forward 15 years. What are the children from these two pastoral families doing? Do they love the Lord, and are they serving Him? Or have they wandered away from God and want nothing to do with church? I think you can figure it out.

We have explored different styles of discipline. It is also important to encourage our children. As plants need water, so do we need encouragement. We need to understand encouragement and apply it responsibly.

CHAPTER 8

THE ART OF ENCOURAGEMENT

Learning the fine art of encouragement is one of the most important skills of effective parenting because children cannot survive without it. There is nothing more encouraging and effective than loving and unconditional acceptance. A healthy self-worth is one of the greatest assets children can have; you can help your children to develop a sense of self-worth. It comes from a sense of belonging, believing that you are capable, and knowing your contributions are valued and worthwhile because you have experienced it.

Someone once claimed, "The deepest principle in human nature is the craving to be appreciated." Another person said, "The art of praising is the beginning of the fine art of pleasing." Encouragement can be as simple as a hug to help children feel and do better.

Jane Nelson related the story of her two-year-old son who had been whining all day and how she felt so annoyed by it. Then she remembered the concept of encouragement. She knelt and gave him a big hug and told him how much she loved him. Not only did he stop whining and crying, but her annoyance also magically disappeared.

Nothing encourages a child more to love life, seek accomplishment, and gain confidence than genuine and sincere praise and reassurance; not flattery, but honest praise and compliments when your children do well. You need to look for little things in which you can encourage your child. We read in Hebrews 3:13, "But encourage one another daily..."

8.1   Encouragement and praise

We all need encouragement— even we as parents! Encourage your children to behave in a respectful and acceptable way. By encouraging them, you provide opportunities for them to develop the perception, "I am capable, I can contribute, and I can influence what happens to me or how I respond." Giving your children a kiss or a hug can serve as encouragement and can help them to do and feel better about themselves. Feeling loved inspires a positive attitude, which can lead to a successful outcome.

The story of how the well-known artist Benjamin West became a painter is inspiring. One day, his mother needed to make a quick trip to the grocery store and left him with his sister, Sally. While she was gone, Benjamin found colored pencils and an ink pot in the cupboard and began to draw a portrait of his sister. When his mother returned, she ignored the ink spatter over the table, leaned over his shoulder and, as she gave him a kiss, exclaimed, "Why, that's Sally!" Benjamin recollected, "My mother's kiss that day— made me a painter!"

A child cannot grow and develop and gain a sense of belonging without encouragement. Half of the job of encouraging a child is found in avoiding discouragement, either by humiliation or by overprotection.

Anything we do that supports a child's lack of faith in himself is discouraging. The other half is grounded in knowing how to encourage. Encouragement is a continuous process aimed at giving children a sense of self-respect and a sense of accomplishment. Right from infancy, they need help to become aware of their place through accomplishments.

Apparently, the author, Walter Scott, was considered a dullard (stupid person) as a child. On many occasions, he was made to sit alone in the corner of the classroom. One evening, his parents entertained several famous literary characters in their home. Among them was the well-known poet, Robert Burns, who noticed a picture on the wall with a couplet (two lines of poetry that rhyme) from a poem. He asked who had written the poem, but no one seemed to know. Then, Walter Scott walked to his side timidly and told him who had written the poem and repeated the rest of the stanza. Burns placed his hand on Scott's head and said: "Ah, Barnie, thou wilt be a great man in Scotland someday." History has it that, from that time on, Walter Scott was a different boy. Years later, he became well-known and was knighted, Sir Walter Scott.

Negative punishment encourages rebellion and is very discouraging for a child. Sometimes children display a vandalizing attitude and break things in or around the house. In a respectful way, inspire them to take pride in fixing and restoring that which was broken; this may discourage them from vandalizing again. When children are encouraged, they feel they belong and start developing responsible behavior. By respectfully encouraging and by setting an example, you can create a warm and inviting atmosphere in the family and encourage each person's strengths.

When praise is used, the individual will repeat that behavior. It involves making a value judgment. Praise is a form of judgment, not facts. It is a positive interpretation of factual data. Judgments can reduce the person's ability to self-evaluate and eventually to make good decisions. It is wise to ask how they think they did. Judgments can be controlling and potentially dangerous. Keep in mind to praise the behavior and not the child.

Even though praise may seem to work, you must consider the long-term effects thereof. The long-term effects of encouragement include self-confidence, and that of praise can be dependence on others. Encourage your children to grow in that which they excel. Praise and encouragement are different concepts; furthermore, they vary a great deal.

8.2 Differences between praise and encourage described by Jane Nelsen in "Positive Discipline" (1996)

Nelson states that *praise* means, "to express a favorable judgment" or "to glorify, especially by attribution and an expression of approval." *Encouragement*, on the other hand, is "to inspire with courage, to spur on, and to stimulate someone." Because the meaning of these two words differs, the effects of both are thus explored.

Praise addresses the doer whereas encouragement focuses on the deed— for example, *good boy* versus good job. Praise only recognizes the complete, perfect product, for instance, "You did it right." When you encourage someone, you encourage the effort and improvement that that person made. You may say, "You gave it your best," or "How do you feel about what you learned?"

When you praise your children, you may patronize and manipulate them to do something like someone else; for instance, you could say, "I like the way Pete is sitting at the table." However, when you encourage, you use respectful, appreciative words such as "Who can show me how we should be sitting at the table?" There is a small difference, but it makes the recipients feel different about themselves.

When you use the *I* message, for example, "I like the way you did the job," you are using praise in a judgmental way. But when you *encourage*, you are more self-disclosing, for instance, "I appreciate your cooperation." Praise is most often used with children when we say, "You are such a good boy." We often use encouragement with adults; when we thank someone for their help, we say, "Thanks for helping."

When we use praise, we often say things such as, "I'm proud of you for getting an A in math." By using this kind of phrase, we may rob children of the ownership of their own achievements. When you encourage, you may say, "That A reflects your hard work." In this way, you give the recipient recognition as well as ownership and responsibility for the effort.

When you praise your children, you invite them to change either for yourselves or for others, whereas, when you encourage, you invite your children to change for themselves. Praise places the locus of control externally: "What do others think?" Encouragement focuses internally: "What do you think?" Praise teaches what to think and suggests evaluation by others; on the other hand, when you encourage, you teach children how to think and to engage in self-evaluation.

The goal of praise is conformity: "You did it right." With encouragement, your goal lends itself toward understanding: "What do you think, feel, or learn?" The effect of praise on self-esteem is that one feels worthwhile only when others approve, while, with encouragement, one feels worthwhile without the approval of others.

8.3   Some guidelines when you give encouragement:
* Encourage children's performances, not their personalities or features.
* Encourage what children are responsible for, not that which they cannot control like the color of their eyes or hair.
* Recognize when encouragement is needed, especially from people who are important to a child.
* Always encourage sincerely. Children know when you are genuine or not.
* Encourage children for what they do when they use their own initiative.
* Keep in mind that the earlier in life encouragement takes place, the better.
* Remember, your attitude and style are as important as your expressions of encouragement.

When you encourage your children, you treat them with respect, and then you can expect respect in return; this will make them respectable grown-ups. Respect is important in all relationships.

8.4   Redirecting misbehavior with encouragement

Look for every child's strength. Sometimes, children who are disruptive have good leadership skills. By encouraging and redirecting their behavior to afford them the opportunity to contribute, you may help them to feel needed. When you encourage their leadership, you enhance that skill. Show respect for and an interest in your children. Let them know that you understand their point of view; this will encourage them, but it does not imply that they can get away with misbehavior.

An excellent way to encourage children is to let them feel useful and that they are contributing. Children feel discouraged when they are misunderstood, humiliated, and/or treated unfairly. They feel some form of blame, shame, and/or pain. When they have tried a skill and have been criticized, they become discouraged. Remember to give your children a few words of appreciation and recognition every day.

Mary's room was always very messy and untidy. One day, her mother asked if she would please help her little sister, whom she loved dearly, to keep her room clean and tidy. She realized that she could not just teach her little sister to be tidy when her room was untidy. This responsibility encouraged Mary to also keep her room neat and tidy. By giving her this responsibility, her mother lessened her work and helped Mary to be responsible and neat!

Spending time with children will encourage them; it makes them feel special. There are times that you can ignore a small behavior problem, but do not allow disrespectful behavior. Take some time to share something of yourself with your children to make them feel that you love and care for them and allow them to believe they are special and important to you.

8.5   Special time

One of the most encouraging things parents can do for their children is to spend special time with them. Small children under the age of two require lots of time. Between the ages of two to six, children need a little less special time. Children between six and twelve do not need too much time, but they still need time to be with family and some special time with their mother and father. During middle childhood, they love to spend time with family and like to please their parents. Make sure that you spend some time alone with each of your children.

The time that you spend together makes the bond between you and your children stronger. Someone once said that love is spelled t-i-m-e; this can help not only with good behavior, but also with cooperation and connecting with you. Special time with a child can have dramatic results. Children feel special when you spend one-on-one time with them and give them special attention.

Tell them something about yourself. If you sometimes ignore a minor offense— they will notice it. This exchange helps children to feel they belong and are significant. Spend time with them before they go to sleep: ask them to share the saddest thing that happened to them that day and then the happiest thing; also share your saddest and happiest events with them, and thank them for sharing their feelings and experiences with you.

8.6   Give encouragement instead of criticism

Parents often do not realize how critical they can be sometimes; criticism can do a great deal of harm to your children, and to your relationship. Ask them questions before you criticize them. Following is some advice from Sonia Spackman:

8.7   When you find fault with your children, ask yourself:

* Why do I criticize? Instead of focusing on their mistakes, focus on their good qualities.

* Does criticizing make you feel better? Criticism is destructive, and they will copy a negative attitude.

* What message does criticism impart? Children think: "If mom or dad thinks I am clumsy, dumb, stupid or lazy, it must be true." They may conclude that they are not acceptable as they are.

* What are the effects of criticism? Criticism damages their self-worth and confidence. Regular criticism turns children away from their parents; they need their parents' love and acceptance. When these important needs are not provided, they feel frustrated, angry, worthless, unloved, and undeserving. They may become overly fearful of criticism, and, when they are grown up, they may become angry and critical, or they may get involved in an abusive relationship.

* What if the criticisms are true? The truth can be destructive and harmful. You will not be wise if you say, "Mary, your hair looks terrible" or "It is your mistake why the team lost." It is not acceptable to say something harmful, even if it might be true.

* How can I tell my children when they are doing wrong? Correction is necessary, but do not do it in a critical manner. If it cannot wait, explain why you are upset, and tell them you will explain why they misbehaved later.

* How do you reason with your children? Two to six-year-old cannot think through a problem logically. They cannot mentally hold two concepts at the same time. Seven to ten-year-old can reason and understand why you are angry, but still need reassurance that you are correcting them because

you love them and want them to behave in a kind, respectful, and responsible way.

* How do I keep from getting angry? Talk to them as you would talk to your good neighbor. You would not yell at your neighbor, "Why did you leave that rake out in your driveway? Put that rake away right now, before I punish you!" Likewise, this is not how you should talk to your children.

Do not say or do anything while correcting your children that will hamper your relationship with them. Your interaction with your children always needs to draw you closer. Try to say, "In the Van Wyk family, we do not swear" or "How do you think we can fix this problem?" When you speak to them like this, you are being sensitive to your children's feelings and focusing on their behavior, not criticizing or blaming them.

You are giving your children the experience to correct their mistakes and build trust and your relationship. Once you have worked through a problem, you forgive and forget; encourage their efforts and celebrate their accomplishments. Criticism instills a little voice in their head— or sometimes a very loud voice— that will criticize them mercilessly for the rest of their lives. Do you want to do that? Criticism is a bad habit and very difficult to break. Do not do it! Encouragement and appreciation are wonderful alternatives to criticism and better for everyone in the whole family. Positive rules in the home will encourage children.

Elora Grace on the web says, criticism makes children feel worst, and it distances you from them; it can cause them to act out to get attention. They can stop trusting you, and it can engage them in risky behaviors. Criticism makes children defensive, and it diminishes their sense of responsibility, ruining the parent-child relationship. It raises emotional state of shame and is not effective. Always try to focus on their positive attributes and actions.

Let us scrutinize how rules in your home can assist you to be respectful and organized. Rules and routines are necessary to have a well-ordered household. It also gives children the feeling that they know what is expected from them.

CHAPTER 9

RULES AND ROUTINE

Rules are found everywhere: at home, at school, at work, on the road, even in a game. When the rules of a game are clear, the players know what is available and can predict with some degree of certainty what the other players will do. Rules organize the game. They reduce uncertainty and anxiety.

A good understanding of and exposure to sound principles is a crucial foundation for good rules. When rules are not developed naturally from principles, children may learn a specific action without seeing or understanding its value. Effective discipline programs provide clear and specific rules along with guidelines for enforcement without sacrificing the higher levels of learning that principles provide. Principles define attitudes and expectations for long-term behavioral growth. Principles are internal guides and values, while rules are made by societies that we live in. Principles are concepts that keep us from killing each other or just being an unpleasant or negative person. Principles drive you to work hard and try to do better in life. They form the core of who you are and will become.

Rules also protect, ensure a child's physical and emotional well-being, and maintain order. They regulate and mediate a child's comings and goings in the world. Children are helpless without them. Paradoxically, a rule is both a limitation and a security of freedom. Some rules are there for you so that you can live safely and consider others.

Every home requires structure and rules; rules give a predictable pattern and help you to make child-rearing easier. They are essential for children; age-appropriate boundaries are necessary to help them to become responsible grown-ups. Without rules, routine, and responsibilities, children cannot be fully secure, cannot have a healthy self-esteem and are not, therefore, free to become all they can be. Rules are the essence of discipline; discipline and love are the cornerstones of security.

Secure children have no desire to misbehave and no need to attract attention to themselves. They are secure, not only because their parents love them, but because they discipline them well. Moreover, their discipline consists of nothing more than a consistent schedule of rules, routine, and responsibilities.

Instead of teaching your children to be obedient, teach them good judgment. Obedience lasts only while you are in the room with them. They need to know what to do in a new and different situation. They will not know what is right or wrong if you have only taught them to obey rules. Our world is complex, and children need to have intelligence and good judgment, not just rules.

Good judgment comes from talking with your children, brainstorming about how they might handle different situations, and discussing moral dilemmas. Connect with your children after they have done something wrong, listen to how they feel about it, and tell them calmly how you feel; this can instill good judgment.

Rules can be communicated in several ways. A direction or instruction is a rule. A task assigned to a child is a rule. Any decision defining what a child may or may not do or have is a rule. A rule which is ill-defined, not enforced, or enforced only sporadically is not a rule. Under this kind of irregular *rule,* a child is a victim and a prisoner of uncertainty. Children will always test a rule; when they experience it as predictable, they are able to function constructively within its limits.

9.1   What rules can do for your children

* Rules prepare children for the real world. They create social
  boundaries; they outline the limits of acceptable behavior
  and preserve the stability of your environment. Rules knit
  society   together.   Rules   are   necessary   for   healthy

development, just as stimulation, good nutrition, and sunshine are.

* Rules teach socialization. Children need to know what is expected of them, and rules provide a framework for that. They show children how to socialize. Some rules teach basic manners like saying, "Please" and "Thank you." After making a request to leave the table or before interrupting someone, teach them to say, "Excuse me, please." Enforce polite words at home.

* Rules provide a sense of order. Rules help a child to predict what will come next like, "Hold my hand when we cross the street" or "Wash your hands before eating." Even little children tend to cooperate better when they know what is required of them, and this develops a sense of belonging.

* Rules make children feel competent and positive. Clear boundaries reduce power struggles. Young children will understand what you want when you formulate your rules positively such as, "You can only eat food in the kitchen or on the back porch."

* When you reinforce a desirable behavior, it can encourage them to cooperate more; for example, say, "Thanks for paying attention while I am talking to you."

* Rules help your children to feel safe. They are designed to protect your children; examples include "No lighting matches" or "Wear a helmet when you ride your bicycle." When your children abide by the safety rules at home, you help them to follow the law in other places, too.

* Rules reassure your children. Too much power can frighten them. They intuitively know that they need their parents to be in charge and they count on you to guide their behavior; for instance, "You are to stay in your bed after I have tucked you in, and, if you come out, you will go to bed a little earlier tomorrow night."

* Rules boost children's confidence. Change the rules as your child gets older. Young children take great pride in achieving simple milestones such as going next door to play with a friend or sleeping over at a friend's house; however, you need to know their friends or the family to whom they are going.

* Family rules go with the family wherever they go. Everyone should behave accordingly, all the time.

* Attach a list of your rules to the refrigerator in your kitchen or where it is convenient for all to see.

9.2   Establishing rules

Have a family meeting, allowing all the members of the family to produce the rules together. If you wish, you can have a rule for safety, one for personal behavior, one for property, and one for neatness. After generating the rules together, make sure that they are upheld; be consistent with the rules you make. This does not mean that you cannot be flexible; you may sometimes, under special circumstances, bend the rules. In making and enforcing rules, always remember rules need to be an act of love. Keep in mind discipline involves teaching and guiding.

When making rules, do not be too strict and restrict your child's behavior. You need to set limits that are in line with your child's developmental level and support his or her natural drive to explore, learn, and practice new skills. They need to be children in the full sense of the word. Do not have too many rules; maintain just a few that are clear and simple for all to understand. Phrase them positively, and clearly explain them so that everybody understands them correctly.

More importantly, make sure everybody abides by them. If you have too many rules, they may become confusing. Rules must reflect your values. Review your rules from time to time to see if they are still relevant. Do they still make sense to everybody in the home?

9.3 Ideas of rules that may be implemented in your home:

* We talk to each other with respect and pleasant voices. We do not yell, hit, or kick. We do not call one another names, nor do we put one another down.

* We care about other people's belongings and ask permission to use something that does not belong to us, and we put them where they belong when we are finished.

* It is everyone's duty to help with the work in our home.

* We always tell the truth and follow directions without complaining. We do not argue with grownups. We may suggest ideas, but they need to be presented in a respectful manner.

* We ask permission before we go somewhere.

* We look for ways to be kind and helpful to each other.

9.4 The last word about rules

State rules briefly, simply, and positively. Do not have too many but stick to the ones you have. Enforce them throughout the day. The smaller your children are the fewer rules you need to have. Rules need to be observable and easy to understand. When your children are older, you can include them in making the rules. It is easier for them to keep the rules that they have helped to create. Rules need to promote learning in a loving environment. Rules are important to the child, and so is routine. Children need to get into a set pattern that will help them to know what is expected of them.

Together with rules, you need to have a schedule for routines. Let us briefly consider routines. Routines are vital in a home to let children know what is going to happen next.

9.5 The Importance of Routine

Routines are to children what walls are to a house; they give their lives boundaries. A well-established routine gives them a feeling of mastery and a sense of order from which freedom grows. They give your children a sense of organization and comfort, help them to behave better, and give them a sense of personal control. They are patterns for living. No child is too young to experience order. Once routine has been established, they will know what to do next.

Routine is important for discipline and gives children security, organizes, and stabilizes their lives, and provides consistency and predictability. Children who are well-disciplined and loved are secure children. Security is a foundation on which children build their self-esteem.

Routine promotes self-control, self-discipline, and self-esteem. It helps them to make sense of their day and to know what to expect and reduces anxiety. Routine can develop a sense of initiative, motivation, resourcefulness, and perseverance which emanate from purpose. Without rules, routine, and responsibility, your children will be unable to develop a completely healthy self-esteem; therefore, they will not become all that they are meant to be.

There are many advantages in giving children chores to do around the house, which you can include in your daily routines. This may take a little longer than if you do it yourself, but the children learn valuable lessons that will last for many years to come. By giving them chores, you teach them the importance of completing an assigned job, and you can use this as an opportunity to emphasize the value of keeping things clean and organized. It sets a pattern of helping around the house and can give children a sense of being part of the household. This makes them feel needed and important.

Children who grow up in a chaotic home where belongings are not put away never learn that life can be more organized. If they grow up in a home where there is no set time or space to do homework, they never learn how to accomplish an unpleasant task. If children do not learn and develop basic self-care routines, they will find it hard to take care of themselves as young adults. Structure allows us to internalize constructive habits.

9.5.1 Inconsistency in childhood routines can have negative effects.

In a study at the University of Albany, it was found that children who had had predictable daily routines as small children had fewer time management and attention problems than those did not grow up with it. The students who had had more consistency in their daily lives as children had better self-control and reduced anxiety and depression as adults.

Dr. Jennifer Malatras, a psychologist at the University of Albany and the study's lead author, told the *Huffington Post*: "Our research suggests greater regularity in family activities and routines is associated with fewer problems overall, and, importantly, we believe it may be possible to improve the regularity of family routines even when it may be less feasible to alter more global aspects of family stability."

She added, "It is important to recognize the complexity of child development and the multiple influences that affect a child's developmental trajectory. Promoting family stability during childhood and adolescence may enhance the development of skills that may be important in promoting adjustment and overall functioning."

9.5.2   How to create a routine
* Create a plan of what your day should be like.
* Draw a chart and stick to it.
* When your children are older, they can help you draw up a schedule.
* It may take a while to get everybody to follow a fixed schedule but keep to your schedule.

* There are times when you may take a break, but make sure to return to the schedule again.
* Revise the schedule from time to time and as your children grow older.
* Do something special each week, something to which they can look forward.
* Have a family meeting once a week to discuss matters related to family dynamics.

In the next section, we will briefly examine a couple of positive approaches to discipline; however, there are many more that you can investigate and develop your own approach by combining a couple of approaches. Raise your child in the best way possible. Always remember that no two children are the same and neither are parents. Each child will need a different approach and your understanding.

CHAPTER 10

A FEW POSITIVE APPROACHES

Guiding principles of positive discipline can be compared to the cement you pour to form a solid foundation when a house is built. These guidelines are necessary; without them, the house would collapse. Guiding principles involve positive disciplining, setting limits, and having standards by which to live. We all need limits and boundaries; your children depend on you to define them because they are too young to define these themselves. They will test these boundaries to see if they are firmly in place.

Jane Nelsen in her book *Positive Discipline* states that positive discipline does not include any blame, shame, or pain as motivators. The purpose of positive discipline is to achieve positive long-range results as well as responsibility and cooperation. It is based on mutual respect and cooperation. It incorporates firmness with dignity and respect as the foundation for teaching life skills.

Equality cannot be equated to the same. Four quarters and a dollar look very different, but they are equal in value. Children are not entitled to all the rights that come with experience, skills, and maturity. However, they do deserve to be treated with dignity and respect. They deserve to develop the life skills they need in an atmosphere of kindness, love, and firmness, and not in an atmosphere of blame, shame, or pain. A positive approach results in a positive outcome!

A positive approach is based on mutual respect and shared responsibility. Children want to experience and be assured that they belong to and have significance in the family. Provide opportunities for them to experience responsibility in direct relationship to the privileges they enjoy. Children need to have responsibilities that are suitable for their age. Haim Ginott (He was a school teacher, a child psychologist and psychotherapist and a parent educator. He pioneered techniques for conversing with children that are still taught today. He was from Tel Aviv Israel) emphasized that communication and the way you talk to your children is the way they will respond to you. He expressed the view that discipline is a series of small victories.

Children do not develop responsibilities when their parents are too strict or controlling; neither can they when their parents are permissive. They learn responsibilities when there is firmness and kindness and when they are treated with dignity and respect. They can learn self-discipline, cooperation, responsibility, resilience, resourcefulness, and problem-solving skills when you involve them and invite them to work with you.

One way to teach children responsibility and other important skills is to have family meetings on a regular basis and to give children an active part in these meetings. There are some guidelines to follow when a family meets together to make it meaningful and interactive.

10.1 Family meetings

A family meeting should be non-threatening wherein all the members of a family meet to discuss matters that are of interest to and affect all. These meetings afford both adults and children opportunities to learn the democratic procedure of cooperation, mutual respect, and social interest. Family meetings are a successful method for enhancing family cooperation and closeness. They provide family values and traditions. A family meeting is *NOT* a platform for lecturing and moralizing but needs to be a pleasant time in which people who love and care about each other socialize.

In a family meeting, each member is treated with respect, and every opinion is heard and discussed. For many families, weekly meetings are a tradition, and provide children with a sense of well-being, self-confidence, significance, and belonging. They also afford family fun, mutual respect, problem-solving experiences, conversations about discipline, and happy memories.

With these meetings, the whole family is involved, and, together, they find solutions and answers. Parents can avoid most problems with their children by suggesting that problems be put on the agenda for the family meeting. This will reduce unpleasant situations. This is also an opportunity to discuss family plans and vacations. It is a time to talk about behavior problems and finding solutions to those issues. There are many benefits for the whole family, including many helpful skills children can learn to equip themselves for school and for real-life situations. Together, the parents and children can produce the rules for the family.

Jane Nelson in her book *Positive Discipline* illustrates a problem in a family and the solution they found. "Jim and Betty each had three children when they got married. The children ranged in age from six to fourteen. Betty was employed outside the home. She loved her new family and wanted to come home to spend time with all of them. However, there was something that was not pleasant for her when she got home. The children would come home from school and leave their books, sweaters, and shoes all over the house. Betty told them that it upset her and that the mess took away her joy. She put the problem on the family meeting agenda. The children came up with a 'safe-deposit box.' The rule was that anything that was left in the common room, such as the living room, family room, and kitchen, could be picked up by anyone who saw it and put in the 'safe-deposit box.' They also decided the item would have to stay there for a week before the owner could claim it. The plan worked beautifully. The clutter problem was solved. If they hadn't stuck to the rules, the whole thing would have been ineffective.

The plan worked because the clutter problem was discussed in a family meeting. The children created the solution, and Mom and Dad did not take over the responsibility. The children saw to it that the rules were enforced. Notice, these rules applied to everyone in the family— both children and parents.

It may take some time for everyone to get used to family meetings, but it is important to remember to stick with the rules. Plan it very carefully until it becomes a habit.

10.1.1 Planning an effective family meeting:

* Family meetings should be held once a week.

* Any family member is allowed to put items on the agenda that will be discussed at the next meeting. Place a piece of paper on the fridge for everyone to consult and add items to.

* The whole family should sit in a circle or around a cleared table so that everybody can see each other.

* It is good to start with appreciation, compliments, acknowledgments, and/or gratitude toward a family member. Alternatively, someone can start the meeting by mentioning something that has touched them.

* Teach your children to say *thank you* after receiving a compliment.

* Only items on the agenda should be discussed at the meeting.

* It is important to stay focused on tasks and work on solving problems.

* Employ brainstorming or role-playing to really understand a problem; then your children will be able to make suggestions on how to solve the particular problem.

* New rules can be made; everybody involved should help make them.

* Consensus should be sought from all present for any decisions passed.

* Meetings may include a review of the next week's activities, planning a family vacation, what chores there are to do, and who will take charge of them.

* End the meeting by planning a fun family activity during the coming week.

* When all the items on the agenda have been discussed, end the meeting by having fun; play a game or share a dessert.

10.1.2 Eight building blocks for successful family meetings:

1. Form a circle or sit around a table.
2. Give compliments and appreciation.
3. Create an agenda during the week before the meeting.
4. Develop communication skills, talking and listening.
5. Learn about distinct realities: we are all unique and have different views.
6. Solve problems through role-playing and brainstorming.
7. Apply logical consequences and non-punitive solutions.
8. Do something special after the meeting.

10.1.3 Benefits from having family meetings

* Children are more motivated to follow rules that they had a part in making.

* They become effective decision-makers when they learn to be contributing members of a family.

* What we do is never as important as how we do it; mistakes are wonderful opportunities to learn.

* The family that meets together once a week gives its children the opportunity to develop strengths   in communication skills, in learning how to talk respectfully to others, and in listening to and giving others an opportunity to speak. They learn to communicate and listen to others.

* The family members learn about individual realities that we are unique and may have varying ideas.

* It helps them to participate and think. They learn how to solve problems and how to find solutions. If the solution

they chose did not work, they need to discuss it again the next week and find another solution.

* Children learn how to debate and how to control themselves.

* They learn brainstorming and other skills that may be useful later in life.

* They learn many social skills which eliminate most discipline problems.

* They learn how to plan and organize events.

* They learn to make healthy decisions.

* They have closer and warmer relationships with one another.

* They develop a higher self-esteem, self-confidence, and a sense of control over their lives.

* They develop a greater sense of personal responsibility and self-discipline.

* They develop positive behaviors and attitudes.

Keep in mind, what you learn as a child, you will take with you through life! Whatever positive style you decide on, family meetings can apply. It can help you to connect to your children and build your relationships.

Rudolph Dreikurs (In - *The New Approach to Discipline*) states, "A misbehaving child is a discouraged child." His approach is thus outlined.

10.2   Rudolph Dreikurs' approach

Dreikurs (1897-1972) was born in Vienna, Austria. He got his medical degree from the University of Vienna and was closely associated with Alfred Adler. He studied family and child counseling and immigrated to the United States in 1937. He later became the director of the Alfred Adler Institute in Chicago and served as professor of psychiatry at Chicago Medical School. Dreikurs explored the underlying causes of children's misbehavior in the classroom, but it can also give you some understanding about your children at home. He is also the author and co-author of many child-rearing books. He has advocated three very strong points in his writings:

* Firstly, children are social beings who want to belong. All their actions reflect their attempts to be significant and to gain acceptance.
* Secondly, children can choose to behave or misbehave. Their behavior is not outside their control.
* Thirdly, children choose to misbehave because they are under the mistaken belief that it will get them the recognition for which they yearn.

Dreikurs called these beliefs mistaken goals. He reminds us to work for improvement, not perfection. Each small improvement is a step forward and a source of further encouragement.

We all want to belong and to have a place to which to belong. Children try to be acknowledged, and, if they do not receive it through socially acceptable ways, they will try *mistaken goals,* which create harmful behavior.

This disruptive behavior reflects the mistaken belief that misbehavior is the only way to receive acknowledgement. Let us explore a summary of Dreikurs' approach outlined in his book *Children, the Challenge.* You may also consult the approaches employed by C.M. Charles in *Building Classroom Discipline*, and Van Wyk in *Positive Discipline: A New Approach to Discipline.*

Dreikurs identifies four mistaken goals: attention-getting, power-seeking, revenge-seeking, and assumed inadequacy. These goals reveal the purpose of the child's misbehavior. If attention-getting fails to gain recognition, children will progress to power-seeking behavior. If that is not rewarded, they will move on to getting revenge, and then they will assume inadequacy. Children are not aware of their mistaken beliefs.

10.2.1 Four mistaken goals of behavior:

Attention– "I belong only when I have attention."

Power– "I belong only when I'm winning or in charge, or at least when I don't let you win."

Revenge– "It hurts that I don't belong, but at least I can hurt back."

Assumed Inadequacy– "I give up. It is impossible to belong."

For each mistaken goal, the child's mistaken belief will be different:

* Attention– "I feel a sense of belonging and significance only if I receive constant attention."

* Power– "I feel a sense of belonging and significance only if I am the boss and do what I want to do."

* Revenge– "I feel hurt because I do not have a sense of belonging or significance, so I have a right to hurt others as I have been hurt."

* Assumed Inadequacy– "I don't feel it is possible to belong and have significance, so I will give up and hope that people will leave me alone."

10.2.2 Two clues that you can use to identify the mistaken goal and help you to break the code:

1. The adult's emotional reaction to the misbehavior, and
2. The child's response when you tell him or her to stop the misbehavior.

10.2.3 The adult's feeling reactions:

1. If you are feeling irritated, worried, guilty, or annoyed, the child's goal is likely to be attention.
2. If you are feeling threatened, challenged, provoked, or defeated, the child's goal is likely to be power. If you

react with power, you will become involved in a power struggle.

3. If you are feeling hurt, disappointed, disbelieving, or disgusted, the child's goal is likely to be revenge. If you cover your primary feeling with anger, you will become involved in a cycle of revenge.

4. If you are feeling inadequate, despairing, hopeless, or helpless, the child's goal is likely   to be assumed inadequacy. If you give in to your feelings, you will be giving up just as the child has.

10.2.4 The child's response when you tell him to stop:

1. Attention: The child stops for a while but resumes the same behavior to get your attention.

2. Power: The child continues misbehaving and passively resists your request to stop. This often escalates to a power struggle.

3. Revenge: The child reacts by doing something destructive or saying something hurtful. This can escalate to a cycle of revenge between you and the child.

4. Assumed inadequacy: The child is passive, hoping you will soon give up and leave him or her alone.

Another interesting approach is the Discipline Quotient developed by Greg Cynaumon. A brief outline of his suggestions follows.

10.3 Discipline quotient factor - DQ

Discipline with love and understanding is essential for effective parenting. Most people are familiar with the IQ (Intelligence Quotient) and EQ (Emotional Quotient). Greg

Cynaumon in *Discover Your Child's DQ Factor* (DQ stands for Discipline Quotient) asserted:

"Misbehaving is just a symptom that your child is feeling insignificant, unimportant, and perhaps unloved." He proposed that you need to look past the symptoms and consider the underlying reason. He explained people do things out of their basic need to feel significant. If your child is feeling inadequate at school or at home, it may be the result of feeling insignificant, insecure, fearful, helpless, hopeless and/or even stupid at times. Give your children responsibilities that will correspond with their age. This will make them feel they are needed and important.

No two children are alike; thus, parents need to understand their children's DQ factor.

According to Cynaumon, there are four areas of needs in children:

1. Some children feel insignificant if they are not in control.

2. They feel insignificant if they cannot get your attention.

3. They gain a sense of significance when they take revenge against the person they want to hurt.

4. They may feel unimportant because they do not have what their friends have.

He suggests that parents use the *FED-UP* (Feelings Experienced During Unruly Periods) test to flesh out their children's DQ motivation. In his research, Cynaumon divided children into four groups, based on the feelings that parents experience most frequently throughout the misbehaving/discipline/resolution process. He used the PERC (Parent's Emotional Response Chart) to determine the child's DQ factor.

* The first DQ is called *Bears.* Here the parents feel threatened, challenged, and angry.

* The second DQ factor is known as Monkeys. The parents feel irritated, annoyed, and controlled.

* The third DQ factor is referred to as Porcupines. Here the parents feel hurt, manipulated, and minimized.

* The fourth DQ factor is called Lambs. Here the parents feel inadequate and frustrated.

He then described some consequences of the children's behavior. He recommended different tests that parents can do to determine their children's DQs.

Becky Bailey proposed another approach: Easy to Love— Difficult to Discipline. Bailey holds a doctorate in psychology: she has concentrated on early childhood education and development. She is the author of numerous research articles and five books.

10.4 Becky Bailey's Easy to Love— Difficult to Discipline

Bailey advocates that you need to change your own behavior before trying to change your children's behavior. When you can control yourself, you become capable of disciplining your children. Self-control means you become aware of your own thoughts and feelings. Without self-control, you turn your life over to people, events, and/or things. You then, consciously, or unconsciously, focus on what other people think and feel about you. Self-control is an act of love and a choice you make each day. You cannot teach what you do not have. You cannot change yourself; you need God's help. Acknowledge what you want to change and ask God to help you. Build respectful relationships with your children and guide them with affection.

10.4.1 Seven powers of Self-Control that parents need to have:

1. The Power of Perception: No one can make you angry without your permission.
2. The Power of Attention: What you focus on, you get more of.
3. The Power of Free Will: The only person you can change is yourself.
4. The Power of Unity: Focus on connecting.
5. The Power of Love: See the best in others.
6. The Power of Acceptance: This moment is as it is.
7. The Power of Intention: Conflict is an opportunity to teach.

She added that parents who act on the Seven Powers for Self-Control and use the Seven Basic Discipline skills model the Seven Values for Living that are necessary for success. Teach your children how to behave, and then hold them accountable for knowing right from wrong. You need to teach them, understand them, and allow them to practice guidelines. Use these powers in times of conflict. In addition, these powers will allow you to look at life through a lens of love rather than a lens of fear. At first, you may feel you are imposing it on them, but, ultimately, they will be internalized and will govern your children from within.

10.4.2 The Basic Discipline Skills grow from each of the seven Powers for Self-Control, and each teaches a value:

SEVEN POWERS FOR SELF-CONTROL	SEVEN BASIC DISCIPLINE SKILLS	SEVEN VAUES FOR LIVING
Power of Perception	Composure	Integrity
Power of Attention	Assertiveness	Respect
Power of Free Will	Choices	Commitment
Power of Unity	Encouragement	Interdependence
Power of Love	Positive Intent	Cooperation
Power of Acceptance	Empathy	Compassion
Power of Intention	Consequences	Responsibility

10.4.3 Each skill has a motto that results in what it should achieve:

1. The Skill of Composure: Living the values you want your child to develop. This teaches integrity.

2. The Skill of Assertiveness: Saying *no* and being heard. This teaches respect.

3. The Skill of Making Choices: Building self-esteem and willpower. This teaches commitment.

4. The Skill of Encouragement: Honoring your children so they can honor you. This teaches interdependence.

5. The Skill of Attributing Positive Intent: Turning resistance into cooperation. This teaches cooperation.

6. The Skill of Empathy: Handling the fusses and the fits. This teaches compassion.

7. The Skill of Consequences: Helping children learn from their mistakes. This teaches responsibility.

If you do not use self-control, you will approach your children unconsciously by manipulating them. However, when you are empowered and use self-control, you will handle situations very differently. The goal is to control yourselves and then structure situations in which children can succeed. These Seven Powers for Self-Control put you in charge of yourself. Change begins with you and extends to your children. Remember that what you focus on, you get more of. Change comes from acceptance, not resistance. Willingness comes from attributing positive intentions to you and to others. Seeing the best in another creates unity, and unity is self-control in action. By learning to discipline yourself, you learn how to guide your children. As you guide your children more effectively, you become more self-disciplined. In this manner, you set an elegant cycle of love in motion.

Discipline is a beautiful concept; it makes our children capable and gives them confidence to live life to the fullest. By your loving guidance, you equip them for life.

Most children have the potential to become successful; by using the significant seven perceptions and skills, you allow your children the strength and empowerment to go from strength to strength.

10.5   The Significant Seven Perceptions and skills

We are born with the potential to become capable; furthermore, we acquire our capabilities primarily through the education we receive from our parents. Children and young people learn from those who have preceded them. When this apprenticeship is adequate, their toolboxes for life are filled with essential tools for successful living.

"As Jesus worked in childhood and youth, mind and body were developed . . . By His own example He taught that it is our duty to be industrious, that our work should be performed with exactness and thoroughness, and that such labor is honorable. The exercise that teaches the hands to be useful and trains the young to bear their share of life's burdens gives physical strength, and develops every faculty. All should find something to do that will be beneficial to themselves and helpful to others. God appointed work as a blessing, and only the diligent worker finds the true glory and joy of life." (DA 72)

Researchers have discovered seven tools that are essential to the parenting process; they are referred to as the *Significant Seven.* Interestingly, researchers discovered these when they were studying failure-- not success. They found that people who were successful in life were characterized by unusual strengths in the Significant Seven. These seven skills are necessary for success throughout one's lifetime.

Nelson, Lott, and Glenn in their book, *Positive Discipline in the Classroom,* state that research has shown that children who have mastered the Significant Seven Perceptions and Skills are at a low risk for all the problems that youth face currently. Those who have grasped these perceptions and skills are unlikely to fall into known problem areas and are likely to prove themselves successful, productive, and capable people.

They discovered that children who do not possess mastery in these perceptions and skills are at high risk for problems of the present-day youth, such as violence, vandalism, drug abuse, teen pregnancy, suicide, low motivation/achievement, and dropping out of school.

10.5.1 The Significant Seven Perceptions

The first three are empowering perceptions; the last four are essential skills.

1. Strong perceptions of personal capabilities: "*I am capable.*"
2. Strong perceptions of significance in primary relationships: "*I contribute in meaningful ways, and I am genuinely needed.*"

3. Strong perceptions of personal power or influence over life: "*I can influence what happens to me.*"

4. Strong intrapersonal skills: *the ability to understand personal emotions and then develop self-discipline and self-control.*

5. Strong interpersonal skills: *the ability to work with others and develop friendships through communicating, cooperating, negotiating, sharing, empathizing, and listening.*

6. Strong systemic skills: *the ability to respond to the limits and consequences of everyday life with responsibility, adaptability, flexibility, and integrity.*

7. Strong judgmental skills: *the ability to use wisdom and evaluate situations to appropriate values.*

Children can develop these perceptions and skills naturally. It happens when parents spend both quality and quantity time with their children. During middle childhood (6-12 years), children love to do things together with the family. When you fix the car, make food, clean the house, or do anything, involve your children by letting them assist you. Take their little hands and guide them with your hand of love. This is how they learn and feel needed. Togetherness builds feelings of belonging.

Togetherness does not just happen; you must plan to spend time together. Giving of yourself is not easy. Take time to talk, listen, and play with your child. Go to places, work together, and share life in a multitude of meaningful ways. Togetherness builds unity, and a sense of love and appreciation for one another. Togetherness says, "*I love you. I like to be with you. You mean so much to me!*" The gift of time gives us a sense of significance, a feeling that we are appreciated, and that we are needed and loved.

It is very negative to say *no* all the time to your children, but you cannot always say *yes* to everything they ask either. However, there are ways to say it differently. Let us look at how you can do it and let your children experience something different.

10.6   Saying NO to your child's requests

*Say **no** when you need to, but do not overdo it.* There are times that you need a positive approach when, for instance, your children do not want to go to bed when it is time, or when your six-year-old begs for a new toy when you are shopping, but you have no intention of buying one.

Unfortunately, moments like these will still occur because we live in an imperfect world, and we are not perfect. According to Renee Kevlis, family therapist, it is much easier to say *no* to a defiant 11-year-old than to a six-foot-tall adolescent who is used to getting his way. If you do not exercise your authority when your children are young, it will be almost impossible to do so later. If you say *no* too often, the word loses its power. Rene Kevlis recommends some possibilities to save your "*no*s" for the times you really need them.

Give choices when you can. When you want your children to clean their room, but they do not want to do it that day, give them a choice: "Would you like to do it before lunch or after lunch?" You will not have to say *no*, but you will insist that their room needs to be cleaned today; however, they are given a choice as to when this will happen. Sometimes, by giving children a little extra leeway, you will be able to avoid a power struggle.

Provide alternatives to what your child is asking for. When your children ask for a cookie and you do not want them to eat between meals or just before dinner time, and they tell you they are hungry, offer an apple or other fruit. If they continue to insist that they do not want an apple, say, "Cookies are not allowed before dinner, but I can offer you fruit or carrot sticks. Which would you like?" By responding in this way, you avoid a flat-out *no*. At the same time, you are helping them understand what an acceptable alternative is.

Assist your children to envision options for themselves. If your children want to go to the pool and ask you to watch them, while you are busy cooking dinner, say to them, "In 20 minutes, I will come to watch you." They may reply that they have nothing to do and are bored. Reply, "What else can you think of that would interest you until I can go outside and watch you?" They may reply, "I cannot think of anything." Then, ask, "What are your three favorite things you like doing when you are by yourself?" If after all of that, they tell you that they do not want to do any of those now, you can say to them, "I will set the timer for 20 minutes, and then I will come. If you can wait, I will be very proud of you."

Helping your children see options is a creative process, one that will aid them in other parts of their lives. When you consistently encourage them to think creatively and look for options, they begin to do this on their own. When you have promised something to your child, always keep your word.

Grant in fantasy what you cannot give in reality. This is a wonderful technique, which was developed by Haim Ginott, a very successful child psychologist. When your child wants a big truck and asks you to buy him one, you may say, "Big trucks are very expensive, and, right now, we cannot afford to buy it for you." He may keep on asking for it. Say to him, "I wish I had all the money in the world so that I could buy the big truck for you and all that you want. I would go right now and buy you two of those big trucks." By granting a request in fantasy what you cannot do, you are letting your children know you understand their desires and would love to grant it if you could. This gives an entirely different message than a flat-out *no*.

It matters how you say *no*. A *no* sounds much harder to accept than a *yes* with a condition. A harsh *no* can activate a reactive state in children to fight, flee, or freeze. In contrast, a supportive *yes* response, even when not permitting a behavior, leads to social engagement, making the brain receptive to what is happening, making learning more likely, and promoting connections with others. This strategy will differ with the age of the child. By saying *yes* with a condition, you are expanding their window of tolerance for not getting their way and giving them practice at delayed gratification. You could also say to them, "I wish I could say yes," or "I wish I could give it to you." You can explain that "There is a lot happening today and tomorrow, so yes, you can invite your friend over, but let us do it on Thursday, then you will have more time with him." That is a lot easier to accept, and it gives a child practice in handling the disappointment and delaying the gratification.

Always follow through on what you say you are going to do. Compromise when you believe it is the best thing to do and mean what you say. Trust your own judgment. However, some things are non-negotiable. There are laws you live by in life and learning how to do this starts when children are young. By being firm, fair, and loving, parents allow their children to grow up to be effective and successful people.

10.7   Natural and logical consequences

It is important to see mistakes as opportunities to learn and to solve problems. You can use natural and logical consequences, instead of punishment. A natural consequence is anything that happens naturally, with no adult interference. When you stand in the rain, you get wet. When you do not eat, you get hungry. When you forget your coat, you get cold. You do not have to say anything because children might realize it naturally from experience. You may show empathy and, in that way, encourage your child.

Logical consequences require the intervention of an adult, usually the parent. It is important to decide what kind of consequence would create a helpful learning experience. It is most effective when children have been involved, in advance, in deciding what consequences would be most effective to help them learn. They can learn a great deal from natural and logical consequences to help them develop responsibility with dignity and respect. It is very important to discuss logical consequences in advance with your children. The following story illustrates this.

Peter, a first grader, forgot his lunch every day. His mother would interrupt her busy schedule to drive to school with his lunch. Then, she applied a consequence. She decided that Peter might learn to remember his lunch if he experienced the consequences of forgetting. She first discussed this with Peter, letting him know she was confident that he could be responsible for remembering his lunch. She also told him she would no longer bring his lunch to school if he forgot it because she knew he could learn from errors.

His mother forgot to talk to his teacher and tell her about her decision, thus, his teacher loaned him money to buy his lunch. Then Peter's mother and teacher met to plan how Peter could learn from his behavior. He called his mother and demanded that she bring his lunch. She kindly, but firmly, reminded him that he could handle the problem. One of his friends gave him half a sandwich. After that, Peter seldom forgot his lunch. When Peter reached the second grade, he added the responsibility of making his own lunch, as well as remembering to take it.

Even though natural consequences are one way to help a child learn the result of behavior, there are times when natural consequences are not practical. These are thus outlined.

1. *When a child is in danger.* Parents cannot allow children to experience the natural consequences of playing in the street. Teach your children never to play in the street. Children need maturity and readiness to learn certain responsibilities. You need to take time to train them while your children are maturing. Take time to train and teach them about dangers every time you cross the street together. Ask your toddlers to look up the street and down the street to see if any cars are coming. Ask them what could happen if they tried to cross the street when a car was approaching. Ask them to let you know when they think it is safe to cross the street. They will learn but will still not be ready for unsupervised play, until they are older.

2. When natural consequences interfere with the rights of others, you cannot allow your child to throw rocks at another person to experience a consequence.

3. When children's behavior does not seem like a problem to them, natural consequences are ineffective. It may not seem like a problem to children if they do not have a bath, do not brush their teeth, fail to do their homework, or eat lots of junk food.

Raising beautiful and happy children requires a balance of wisdom and judgment. You can trust yourselves to make good decisions about disciplining your children when your actions are guided by love, compassion, fairness, respect, and integrity. Treat your children as guests in your home and enjoy them! Proverbs 22:6, thus explains it: "Start a child on the right path while he's young, and, when he is old, he'll not forget what he's been taught."

Remember that discipline is a lifelong journey-- an act of love; it is not a technique; there is no success recipe for it. Also, remember that you can connect to your child, work on it, and enjoy it!

CHAPTER 11

CONNECTING WITH YOUR CHILDREN

This approach is all about connecting and actively guiding your children to grow lovingly, compassionately, and spiritually. When you are the model in all that you wish your children to develop in and grow to maturity, you will enjoy your children and help their brain to develop in a beautiful way.

Families need to connect and have a healthy relationship with each other. A loving connection wires the brain for a desire to do the right things. It lets children move beyond power struggles, helps them to cooperate, and nurtures forgiveness. The connected family is one in which every member is empowered, has their needs met, and has a voice that is heard. There is no coercion, fear and/or external rewards, but intrinsic motivation, helpfulness and problem-solving. In a connected home, parents guide their children with love, and they help them to be successful, obey the rules, and have routines and discipline structures.

Some positive approaches have already been outlined. I now want to introduce you to another positive approach, namely, that of Daniel Siegel and Tina Payne Bryson, which is described in their book, *No-Drama Discipline*.

11.1   No-drama discipline
According to Siegel and Bryson, before you respond to your children's misbehavior, ask yourself three questions:

1)   Why did my child act this way?

Look at the situation, and realize your children were trying to express something, but did not handle it correctly. When you understand why they misbehaved, you can respond more effectively and with compassion.

2)   What lesson do I want to teach at this moment?

Discipline is not giving a consequence or punishment but teaching a lesson, whether it is about self-control, or sharing, acting responsibly, or whatever needs to be taught.

3) How can I best teach this lesson?

Keep your child's age and the context of the situation in mind. Ask yourself, "Was there a reason for spilling the milk when he took it out of the fridge? Was it possibly too high for him to reach?" Think of how to express yourself to make your message effective. There are more effective and loving ways to help them understand what you are trying to teach them.

When you ask these questions, you will respond differently. You can teach a long-lasting lesson and skill, build character, and prepare children for making good decisions in the future. Each child is different and needs a different reaction from you. In the beginning, this may take some time, but, as you practice, it will become easier. It is always better to try to see things from your children's perspective, and remember they need your guidance.

By reacting lovingly and with empathy, you are shaping their brain, so that they can make better decisions—subsequently, you will understand them better, and strengthen your relationship. It is possible for experiences to change your children's brains! Siegel and Bryson compare the brain to a two-story building, with an upstairs and a downstairs.

11.2 The upstairs and downstairs brain

Siegel and Bryson compared the brain to a house, with a downstairs and an upstairs level. The downstairs brain includes the lower parts, the brain stem, and the limbic region; these parts are well-developed at birth. They are responsible for basic functions, such as breathing, digesting, blinking; for inborn reactions and impulses, such as fight and flight; for strong emotions, such as anger and fear; and instincts, such as protecting yourself, regulating sleep and wake cycles, and digestion. It is the downstairs brain that causes toddlers to throw a toy or bite someone when they do not get their way.

The upstairs brain is different. It is responsible for more sophisticated and complex thinking; it keeps developing until we are in our mid-20's. This part is undeveloped at birth and starts to develop during infancy. It is made up of the cerebral cortex, which is the outermost layer of the brain, directly behind the forehead, continuing to the back of the head, like a half dome. Here more intricate mental processes take place, such as thinking, imagining, planning, and relational skills that allow us to live a balanced, meaningful life, and enjoy healthy relationships.

Our brains can change and are changeable; they can be molded intentionally by experiences. Studies have shown that, when children learn the fundamentals of playing the piano, their brains develop differently from the brains of children who do not play it. These children understand their own bodies in relationship to the objects around them better. Mindfulness exercises can result in changes in the brain's connections that can significantly affect how well a person interacts with other people and adapts to difficult situations.

Experiences that are repeated change the brain physically. Be intentional about those experiences you wish your child to display. Everything they see, hear, feel, touch, or even smell, influences their brain and the way they view and interact with their world-- their family, neighbors, strangers, friends and classmates. All these have an influence on them. When neurons fire simultaneously from experiences, they become connected and form a network. When an experience is repeated over and over, it strengthens the connections among those neurons; when they fire together, they wire together!

A positive experience with a music teacher can lead to neural connections that links music with pleasure and a good feeling of accomplishment. However, the opposite is equally true. A negative experience with a harsh instructor can result in connections in the brain that create an obstacle to enjoyment in general.

When children are at their worst, be there for them. Demonstrate that you understand that they are having a hard time. A loving, sensitive, and connecting discipline allows children to feel safe. It helps them to make better decisions, to understand what they feel, and, also, to consider other people's perspectives as well as their own. A feeling of safety also allows them to act responsibly. However, when you focus on control and fear, you undermine their feelings of safety.

By using loving discipline, you strengthen the connections, and integrate the upstairs and downstairs brain. These connections lead to personal insight, responsibility, flexible decision-making, empathy, and morality. Your actions determine what kind of people your children will become. Give your children choices, and ask them how they think they should act, rather than telling them what to do.

This will help them to learn how to make positive and productive choices on their own. Let them practice choices and thereby build important skills that will be wired into the brain.

11.3   From tantrum to tranquility

Siegel and Bryson state that connecting with your children should be the first step when you discipline because it allows effective learning to occur. Connecting is such a powerful tool when your children are upset. Practice being proactive; this can make all the difference. Be there for your children when they are hungry, angry, lonely, and tired, or feel angry, dejected, ashamed, embarrassed, overwhelmed, and/or out of control. Let them feel loved and accepted by connecting to them, then you can soothe their internal storm and help them to calm down. By connecting with them, you move them out of a reactive state into a receptive state.

Ask yourself, "Is my child ready to hear me, ready to learn, ready to understand?" Without connection, emotions can spiral out of control. Connection calms, allowing children to regain control of their emotions. Empathy soothes the feeling of isolation or being misunderstood, which influences the downstairs brain. However, with connection, they can make thoughtful choices and handle themselves better because connection integrates the brain.

Siegel and Bryson explain integration by using the image of a river of well-being. They require you, the reader, to imagine that you are in a canoe, floating along in a peaceful river. You feel calm, relaxed, and ready to deal with whatever comes your way. This does not mean that everything is perfect but that you are in an integrated state of mind-- calm, receptive, and balanced.

Sometimes, children are not able to stay in the flow of the river. They find themselves on either side of the river. The one side of the river represents chaos, where dangerous rapids make life uncontrollable. Near the chaotic bank, they are easily upset by minor obstacles or overwhelmed by their emotions, such as anxiety or intense anger, which can make them feel chaotic.

The other side of the river represents rigidity. Your children may feel that they cannot compromise or negotiate in any meaningful way. With chaos on the one side and rigidity on the other, children are offered neither control nor flexibility. They both keep them out of the peaceful flow of the river of well-being. Whether they are chaotic or rigid, they are not able enjoy emotional health or feel at ease with the world.

When you connect with your children, they move back into the flow, where they experience a sense of balance and feel better. Connecting starts when you listen, talk, and show nonverbal empathy. You are reaching their feelings, thoughts, and perceptions, which gives meaning to them. You can lovingly touch them, rub their back, or give a warm hug; it will make them feel good and decrease their stress.

Connecting builds their brains, and improves relationships, self-control, empathy, and personal insight. When you offer comfort when they are upset, listen to their feelings, and love them, even when they have misbehaved, you significantly affect the way their brain develops and the kind of people they will become. Connections strengthen the connective fibers between the upstairs and downstairs brain so that the upper parts of the brain can communicate with the lower brain more effectively. You move them from reactivity to receptivity and build the brain. Furthermore, you deepen the bond between you and your child.

When you notice a tantrum, see it as an opportunity to make your children feel safe and loved. It will give you a chance to soothe their distress. Always respond with empathy. When children throw a tantrum, their young developing brains are becoming disintegrated, and their immense emotions take over. When you show understanding, you are going to offer a much more compassionate response when they are screaming, yelling, and kicking. Showing empathy and compassion will calm them rather than viewing them as being difficult or naughty.

Do not ignore children when they have a tantrum because they are miserable and suffering. They need you to be with them and provide reassurance and comfort. You need to be calm, loving, nurturing, and connect with them.

Set boundaries by not giving in or letting your children harm themselves, destroy things, or put others at risk. Set limits while communicating your love and walking through difficult moments with them. Say, "I am here." Remember your primary goal is to connect! You are not spoiling your children because spoiling is not about how much love, time, or attention you give your children. You cannot spoil them by giving them too much of yourself. You cannot spoil your infants by holding them too much or responding to their needs. If you do not respond or sooth them, you will assist them to become insecurely attached and anxious. They are entitled to your love and affection.

When you are sensitive, you give your children resources, resilience, and relational skills. They need to learn that relationships flourish with respect, nurturing, warmth, consideration, cooperation, and compromise. When children feel seen, safe, and soothed, they feel secure and thrive. When your children are at their worst, they need you most! Share in their experience, connect, and allow them to move back into the river of well-being.

11.4   Connect first

By connecting with your children, you influence them in a positive way. Connection creates a sense of safety and openness, but punishment, lecturing, nagging, scolding, blaming, or shaming create fight, flight, or freeze in your children. Pause for a while, be calm and think-- this will help you to be wise in a difficult moment so that a connection can occur. Connection has many benefits. A short-term benefit is that it moves children from reactivity to receptivity. The long-term benefit is that it builds their brain. The relational benefit involves deepening your relationship.

11.5   Some connecting principles that can guide you in connecting with your children:

1. Turn down the Shark music.

Siegel and Bryson refer to toxic background music. Background music is what you feel reactive about or when you respond to something from the past. It makes you act with fear. When you connect with your children, you need to pay attention to them, and let go of the background noise caused by past experiences and future fears. Always be very careful what you do and how you speak. Let go of the fears, expectations, and reactivity that keep you from looking at the situation, and rather respond with love.

2. Chase the *why*

Shark music lets you make assumptions about what you perceive, but it will obstruct the connection. Ask yourself, "Why are my children doing this?" Address the behavior and find out what caused it. When you only address the behavior, you concentrate on the symptoms and not the reason your children misbehaved. When you find the reason for their behavior, it can help you to understand what is going on with your children.

3. Think about the *how*

What and how you say it is very important. How you say it is what your children feel about you and themselves, and how they will treat others. They will cooperate faster when they feel connected and when you engage them in a pleasant and playful way. Also, always try to discipline respectfully, playfully, and calmly. Connecting is a four-part process.

11.6 The four-part process of connecting

Each child and each parent is different; however, connection may be viewed as a four-part process. Connecting is a step-by-step development. It may not always follow the exact same order, but the strategies are the same.

1. Communicate comfort.

Words are needed to validate feelings, but more important is what takes place nonverbally. You can communicate so much without ever saying a word. A loving touch is comforting, so put your hand on their arm, pull them close to you, rub their back, hold their hand, or give them a warm hug. This will alter their brain chemistry and help you to connect, even during moments of high stress. When you discipline your children, make sure you are relaxed and in a nonthreatening posture; get down to their level. This will calm you and your child. Your posture can send all kinds of messages, especially when you cross your arms, shake your head, or roll your eyes. Nonverbal messages betray you, and your child will believe the nonverbal over the verbal because the nonverbal is more powerful.

2. Validate.

Embrace their feelings and connect. Your children need to know that you are with them in the middle of all those massive feelings. Tune in to them. This will help them calm down and feel understood and loved. Say something like: "That really made you sad, didn't it?" or "I can see you feel left out," or even "You are having a hard time." To identify and name the emotion is a powerful response when children are upset. It also gives them vocabulary so they can recognize what they are feeling and understand their emotions. You may say, "I get it, I understand. I see why you feel this way." To you, it may seem small and insignificant, but they experience it as very real. Attune, acknowledge, and identify what they are feeling; by doing this, you validate their feelings.

3. Stop talking and listen.

Listen and observe to understand what your children are communicating. Are they hurt, disappointed, or angry? Is the logical part of their upstairs brain not functioning? Communicate comfort and validate their feelings. Say, "It really hurts that you didn't get invited, doesn't it? I would feel left out, too." Stop talking and listen to what they are saying. Listen to their feelings, focus on their emotions, and let go of the shark music that prevents you from being fully present with them in that moment. Sit down and let them express themselves.

4. Reflect what you hear.

After listening to your children, reflect on what you have heard. This communicates comfort. Now, you can focus on what your children have told you. Say to them, "I can tell how mad you were." It is healing to feel understood. You tell them what you heard: "I hear what you are saying, you really hated it when I told you that you had to leave the party," or "No wonder that made you mad; I would have felt angry, too." You defuse their high emotions, communicate comfort, and convey compassion by getting below their eye level, hold them, or rub their back; also, make facial expressions that convey empathy. You will thus validate their experience. You may say, "I know-- I know you are really upset." They may respond, "Yes, and I hate Pete!"

Now, reflect to them what they are feeling, but you do not want to reinforce in their mind that they hate Pete. This calls for some careful tiptoeing so that you can be honest with your children and help them better understand their feelings. You may say something like, "I don't blame you for being so mad. I hate it when people tease me like that, too. I know you love Pete and that you two were having so much fun together, just a few minutes ago, when you were playing with the wagon. But you are mad at him right now, aren't you?" The goal with this type of reflecting is to make sure your children comprehend that you understand their experience, and, in doing so, you will soothe their heavy emotions. However, do not allow a feeling that is a momentary state; their anger with Pete is to be perceived in their mind as a permanent trait that is an inherent part of their relationship. That is why you need to give them perspective and remind them of the fun they had with the wagon or whatever they were playing with.

Siegel and Bryson state that the advantage of reflecting your children's feelings is that it communicates that they have not only your love, but your attention as well. Brain studies (Sources?) have shown that the experience of physical pain and the experience of relational pain, such as rejection, look very similar in terms of location of brain activity. Thus, when you give your children attention and focus on what they are doing and feeling, you meet an important relational and emotional need. They then feel deeply connected and comforted, and this communicates your love and prepares them for redirection after you have connected.

11.7 After connecting, redirect.

After you have connected, you redirect. Let us explore how you can redirect them toward using their upstairs brain so they can make more appropriate decisions that becomes second nature with time.

Neurons that wire together fire together. Discipline is concerned with teaching to optimize learning. There are two principles to guide you in what to do. Ask what lesson you want to teach and how you can best teach it. The two principles are:

1. Wait until you and your child are ready.

When you have connected and allowed your children to come to a place where they are ready to listen and use their upstairs brain, then it is time to redirect. Address the behavioral issue as soon as possible, but only when your child is in a calm, receptive state of mind, even if you need to wait. You can begin by saying, "I would like to talk about what happened yesterday at bedtime. That did not go so well, did it?" Siegel and Bryson state that waiting for the right time is essential when it comes to teaching effectively. Never redirect if either your child or you are not ready. When you are ready, create an environment where your child is calm, alert, and receptive.

2. Be consistent, but not rigid.

When you are consistent, your children know what you expect of them and what they can expect from you. Children need consistency, but not rigidity. This kind of predictable, sensitive, attuned care is what builds secure attachment. This gives them a secure base and clear boundaries when their emotions are exploding. Rigidity is fear-based. Their physical safety is not negotiable, but they also know that, at times, you will consider all the factors involved carefully. You want to respond to a situation in a way that works best for them and for the entire family, even if that means making an exception.

11.8   Three outcomes of mindsight

Mindsight is the ability to see your own mind and the mind of another. It allows you to develop meaningful relationships while keeping a healthy and independent sense of self. By asking your children to consider their own feelings while also imagining how someone else might feel about the situation, you help them to develop mindsight.

Let us look at the three outcomes of redirecting. When integration does not occur, chaos or rigidity results. When a relationship breaks down because you do not honor each other's differences or when you do not link compassionately to each other, integration is violated. There are a few steps to repair a situation and make things right when you make a bad decision or hurt someone with your words or actions. Let us briefly look at each of these outcomes:

Outcome # 1 - Insight:

Guide your children to develop insight and vocabulary about their feelings; this will allow them to understand what they are feeling and to have more control over their reactions when they experience a difficult situation. Ask them to reflect on their feelings and reactions. Name the emotions you observe. When children gain insight into themselves, understand the results of the reflective conversations: they are then able to cultivate mindsight.

Outcome # 2 Empathy:

Assist your children to reflect on how their actions affect others. Their insight helps them to develop empathy. This repeated focus of attention on the inner mental life changes the wiring in the brain and strengthens the part of the upstairs brain that shows empathy. When your children can see things from another person's point of view, they develop an awareness of other people's feelings. Practice in this will allow them to display empathy and care. As insight and empathy develop, the foundation for morality and integration is laid.

Option #3 - Integration and the repair of ruptures:

To develop your children's upstairs brain, ask them how they can repair a situation and what positive steps they can take. Repair builds insight and empathy, and, subsequently, mindsight. Making things right is never easy for anybody. When they learn to know themselves better and consider other people's feelings, they will be able to act toward repairing the situation, build and strengthen connections within the frontal lobe, which will help them to understand themselves and get along with others as they enter adolescence and adulthood.

11.9   Some redirecting strategies

Siegel and Bryson suggest that, before you redirect, be calm and connect with your children, and then use the disciplinary moment to address their behavior and guide them to make better choices. Before doing anything, make sure you are ready, and your children are ready. Your response will have a great impact on how successful you will be.

Be calm, loving, and nurturing while you discipline your children. A kind tone of voice can be powerful as you initiate a conversation about the behavior you are wanting to change. Be firm and consistent in your discipline, but interact and communicate warmth, love, respect, and compassion. Do not dismiss your child's feelings. When you make a statement like, "It is not a big deal," or "Why are you so upset about it?" you minimize children's experiences, their thoughts, feelings, and desires. It is more effective to listen, empathize, and truly understand your children's experiences before you respond. Your children's desires might seem absurd to you, but never forget, they are very real and important to them. Do not disregard something that is important to them. After connecting, redirect them back to their upstairs brain.

Parents have found the following strategies most helpful. Choose the ones that make sense in your various circumstances.

Consider your children's temperament, age, and developmental stage as well as your own parenting philosophy.

Strategies to redirect children when they have completely lost control of themselves follow.

11.9.1   An acronym of strategies to redirect:
Reduce words.
Embrace emotions.
Describe, do not preach.
Involve your child in the discipline.
Reframe a *no* into a *yes* with a condition.
Emphasize the positive.
Creatively approach the situation.
Teach mindsight tools.

1 Reduce words.

Older children know when they have done something wrong and do not want a long lecture about their mistakes. Resist the urge to over-talk. Address the issue and teach the lesson. Children do not want long lectures on what they did wrong. When addressing your toddler's misbehavior, connect and address the feelings behind the behavior. Then address the behavior, give them alternatives, and move on.

2 Embrace emotions.

Assist your children to differentiate between their feelings and their actions. Guide them to understand that feelings are neither good nor bad; they simply are. There is nothing wrong with getting angry, being sad, and/or feeling frustrated and that they want to destroy something. Let them know, "You can feel your feelings, but you cannot do what you want to do." Say *yes* to feelings, and *no* to inappropriate behavior.

When your children repeatedly hear, "Stop crying" or "Why are you so upset? "Everyone else is having fun," they are going to doubt their ability to accurately comprehend what is going on inside of them. They will be confused, full of self-doubt, and disconnected from their emotions. As they become adults, they may often feel their emotions are unjustified. They may doubt their subjective experiences and even have a hard time knowing what they want and feel at times. Embrace your children's emotions and offer a response when they are upset or out of control. Let them know you are there for them, you will always listen to how they feel, and they can come to you to discuss anything that troubles them.

3 Describe, do not preach.

Describe what you see when your children misbehave; they will understand what you are saying. With a toddler, you could say, "You are throwing the pieces of puzzle, that makes it hard to put it all together." When addressing older children, you could say, "I see the dishes are still in the sink," or "That sounds like very mean words you are saying to your brother." By simply stating what you see, you initiate a dialogue with them, which opens the door to cooperation; this is a better teacher than an immediate reprimanding. Instead of demanding, describe what you see!

4 Involve your child in the discipline.

By involving your children in the discipline, they will feel more respected and be willing to cooperate and find solutions to the problem. They might come up with great ideas that you have not even considered. Ask them what they can do differently next time they get upset. Ask what you can do to help them calm down. This type of conversation will develop their understanding and the importance of regulating emotions, honoring relationships, planning, and expressing themselves properly. By doing this, you will strengthen your relationship, and they may be able to handle themselves better in the future.

5 Reframe a *no* into a conditional *yes*.

It matters how you say *no*. A *no* sounds much harder to accept than a *yes* with a condition. A harsh *no* can activate a reactive state in children to fight, flee, or freeze. In contrast, a supportive *yes* response, even when not permitting a behavior, leads to social engagement, making the brain receptive to what is happening, making learning more likely, and promoting connections with others.

This strategy will differ with the age of the child. By saying *yes* with a condition, you are expanding their window of tolerance for not getting their way and giving them practice at delaying gratification. You could also say to them, "I wish I could say yes," or "I wish I could give it to you." You can explain that "There is a lot happening today and tomorrow, so *yes*, you can invite your friend over, but let us do it on Thursday when you will have more time with him." That is a lot easier to accept, and it gives a child practice in handling the disappointment and delaying gratification.

Pay attention to your tone of voice. You can negotiate with your children. Compromise is not a sign of weakness; it is evidence of respect for your children and their desires. In addition, it gives them an opportunity to think, equipping them with important skills about considering, not only what they want, but also what others want, and then formulating fair arguments based on that information.

6 Emphasize the positive.

One of the best ways to deal with misbehavior is to focus on the positive aspects of what your children are doing. Instead of focusing on the problem, emphasize the positive. Encourage good behavior and point out what you like about them and when they are obedient. Say positive comments, such as, "I love it when you are encouraging your sister to be neat. Thanks for thinking ahead and helping me with this project," or "I love seeing you two have so much fun together." There are times that you will need to address negative behaviors but try to focus on the positive and allow them to understand that you notice and appreciate it when they make good decisions and handle themselves well.

7 Creatively approach the situation.

Be creative and ready because each situation needs a different approach. Come up with different ways to handle an issue. Instead of demanding, be creative and playful. Humor and silliness can be very effective in discipline moments. Be respectful in your sense of humor as this can communicate that it is not a threat, but it helps to connect with your children. Be more receptive and give your full attention. Creativity comes in handy in all kinds of other ways, too. Avoid a fight, have fun, and be playful. By being creative with your solutions, you will all enjoy your relationships more.

8 Teach mindsight tools.

Mindsight is seeing your own mind as well as other people's minds, and it promotes integration. When your children have developed insight, they can learn to use that insight to handle difficult situations. They can use their minds to take charge of how they feel and how to act. Practice and let them tell you how they feel and see the world.

11.9.2 Apply self-control and strategies to reason.

In the Stanford marshmallow experiment during the 1960s and 1970s, young children were brought into a room, one at a time. The researcher invited them to sit at a table with a marshmallow on it. He explained that he would leave the room for a few minutes. If the child resisted the temptation to eat the marshmallow while he was gone, he would give the child two marshmallows when he returned. This study demonstrated self-control and applying strategic reasoning. They found that children who demonstrated the ability to wait longer before eating marshmallow tended to have many improved life outcomes as they grew up. They did better in school, scored higher on the SAT, and were physically fitter.

Researchers then taught some children mindsight. They found when they provided the children with mental tools that gave them a strategy to assist them not to eat the marshmallow, it helped them manage their emotions and desires. These children were more successful at demonstrating self-control. When they told some children to imagine that it was just a picture of a marshmallow, they could wait longer than the children who were not given any strategies to help them to wait.

Assist your children not only to feel their feelings and sense their sensations, but to notice how their bodies feel and witness their own emotions. For instance, when they notice that they are feeling sad, it may not be the size of a grape, but like a watermelon. Siegel and Bryson described it like being an actor, experiencing the scene, but also being the director who watches more objectively and can see from outside the scene to have more insight about what is taking place on the inside. The child may say, "I hate tests! My heart is pounding, and I am starting to freak out!" But then, he may also observe, "I really want to do well, so I will not watch television. I will put in some extra time to learn, so that I can do better."

Encourage your children to feel their feelings and ask them to share them with you. Give your children perspective and help them understand that they can focus their attention on other aspects of their reality. With this, they will be able to see the world differently and feel better. When you teach your children mindsight, you give them the gift of being able to regulate their emotions, rather than being ruled by them. By this, they do not have to be victims of their environment or their emotions.

Remember to connect before you redirect. In this way, you will be able to achieve the primary goals of discipline: gaining cooperation and building your children's brains. This will help them to be kind and responsible people who enjoy successful relationships and meaningful lives.

If you want to change the way you have been parenting or are new parents who are expecting a child, think and plan intentionally to do the best in teaching and guiding your children. Keep in mind, when children feel connected, they also feel they belong and have significance.

CHAPTER 12

RETHINK THE WAY YOU DISCIPLINE

Janusz Korczak stated, "There are many terrible things in this world, but the worst is when a child is afraid of his father, mother, or teacher. He fears them, instead of loving and trusting them." Janusz Korczak was the pen name of Henryk Goldszmit, a Polish Jewish doctor and author. Goldszmit— a trained pediatrician-- first gained fame in the early 1900s writing storybooks for children and childcare books for adults. He developed groundbreaking views on raising children, urging adults to treat them with both love and respect. As his reputation as an author grew, Goldszmit became known throughout Poland as Janusz Korczak.

Be respectful to your little ones when you guide and direct them. Respectfulness can be easy. Do not punish or threaten your children when they are out of control; rather connect and love them. Closeness, playfulness, and emotional understanding are far better ways than punishment. Change your brain and your child's brain by changing the circumstances in your home.

It is so easy to have an outburst when your children do something that upsets you. Take a break in the heat of the moment and wait for things to settle down before you discipline! Talk to someone; it may help you to cool off. Talking to others will enable you to unload your feelings; this will make discipline easier.

Cool off and connect with your children. Sit on the couch, play, and put your arms around them. Be aware of your children's feelings and needs. Instead of punishment, get to know your children, set clear limits, and make sure they understand what you are saying. Kay Kuzma talks about the "love cup" Think of when you last played together or just had some time together. Is your child's love cup empty? Is that why he or she is acting this way? Is your love cup empty? Reconnecting might require a hug, some quiet time together, wrestling or running around outside, or having a snack or a talk. You can also sit on the couch and have a one-on-one meeting. Meetings on the couch can build connections and empower both your children and you.

12.1 Choose a "meeting on the couch" instead of "time-out."

Lawrence Cohen, who wrote *Playful Parenting*, expressed the view that you need to connect with your children. It can make a big difference if you change the scene and connect. Tensions go away and frustrations disappear when you sit down and have some fun, talking and lovingly touching your children.

A meeting on the couch is very different from time-out because there is no power struggle about how many minutes are left, and no dragging children who kick and scream into their room. Sitting on the couch is something you do together! Sitting on the couch is not just for misbehavior; it can happen anytime, and it can be to connect, or just to strengthen the connecting bond. You can call a meeting on the couch when you see your child is sad or irritable, when you have not connected for a while, to plan an event, or when you see his cup is nearly empty. A meeting on the couch makes everyone feel better and fills up the "love cup."

Cohen stated time-outs may work in a positive way; if children have a cozy place where they can go to calm down when they choose to go— not when the parent chooses to send them. He added that, in most homes, time-outs are used as a punishment. Sometimes, the parent and the child need time-outs to cool off before one explodes, and it is better to stop a conflict before it gets out of hand. This kind of time-out is not punishment. Time-outs are torture for most children. Children need contact as they are afraid of separation and exclusion. When you give your children attention, they will not be desperate for it. To connect with your children, you need their attention. Once you have their attention, and a real connection, you will get real cooperation.

12.2 Teach, play and employ good judgment.

It is fun to play and fill your day with laughter. Laughter can be a sign of connection between people, a sign of successfully completing a challenging task, or a sign that a child no longer feels miserable or hurt. Laughter brings people together, and it is a way to release fears, embarrassment, or anxiety. Make it a habit to use play, fun and laughter when you parent— this will make parenting less of a challenge.

Cohen states that, when your children are bored, or you have battles over dessert or bedtime, play a game, play dessert, play bedtime. If you have trouble with back-talk, pick up two dolls and have one talk back to the other. Instead of repeating, "You must get dressed right now," try saying, "There is only one rule: You can't wear one red shoe and one black shoe!" Cohen explained this will help them to be more cooperative. A playful approach to discipline is healthy.

With the busy schedules that we all have, you may often punish, and forget discipline is to teach! You know how one-year-olds drop food off the side of their highchair— they are learning about gravity. Do not punish their first science experiments! Little ones do not know they are being philosophers and scientists. Children learn about things through play, and, when you can master the skill to be playful about learning (disciplining), you have mastered something great!

When you punish, you are not helping your children to be loving people. When you are loving and affectionate, have high moral standards and have a close relationship with them, it can help your children to become thoughtful, considerate, honest, kind, and loving grownups. Close connections are very important to your children. It makes sense to use love and communication to discipline.

12.3 Be aware of your children's feelings and needs.

When toddlers start pulling everything off the counter, they may be saying, "I need something to do, and I want somebody to do it with me." If an eighth grader starts forgetting to do his homework, he may be saying, "I fear high school coming up: I am not sure if I am ready." You may not always be right about your interpretation, but it is helpful to try to discover the underlying feeling regarding every behavior that troubles you.

> Cohen proposed some common interpretations that fit many problem situations:
> * You are bored; you must be feeling lonely. Let us play a game, or we can invite someone over.
> * I can see you are starting to get discouraged, so I am going to give you encouragement.
> * You and I have not had much time together, so let us do something special.
> * You seem sad, so I am going to comfort you.
> * You need more room to run around and get rid of some of your energy. Let's go outside.
> * You seem mad, so I am going to hold a big pillow so you can whack it.
> * You have been trying to get my attention, so I will give you my undivided attention.
> * You seem too fidgety to sit still. Let's dance!
> * You seem overwhelmed. I am going to help you calm down. Let us take three deep breaths together.
> * You have been very mean toward your brother; I would like to hear about what is bothering you.

* You seem cranky and irritable. Let us have a snack and see if that helps.

Children who misbehave are looking for love and comfort, not punishment. Connect with them and focus on the underlying need and feeling. Babies can die or get sick if they are not loved. We all need love, and we need each other— your children need to feel your love. Prevent misbehavior when you see it coming. Interrupting destructive behavior is setting a limit and not punishment. Limits help children gain control and express their feelings. A lonely child needs to develop some friendships.

12.4 Instead of punishing— prevent it and know your child.

Effective discipline leads to a connection and a conversation whereas an ineffective discipline leads to shame and separation. Stay engaged with your children. Harshness and coldness lead to isolation and powerlessness in children. Make eye contact, talk softly, hold them gently, and, when you are angry, take a deep breath. Remember to play with them. The more you play with them and maintain closeness, the less you will need to discipline.

Punishment slows development down. Some parents, without realizing it, can punish children for being different than they think they should be. You like to do everything fast; they dawdle. You sit quietly; they fidget. Their room is messy; you want it to be neat. You like it quiet; they like it loud. You like it calm; they like it wild. Punishment cannot change a child's temperament; we are all different, and so is your child!

Get to know your children and how they respond to different types of discipline. What works for one child may not work for another one. Keep in mind that all children are frightened by discipline that is too strict or severe. All children need guidance and structure, which needs to be applied lovingly and in a relaxed manner, never in anger or revenge.

CHAPTER 13

PLAY WITH YOUR CHILDREN

Playing with your children is very important and can mean the world to them as well as to you. Lawrence J. Cohen wrote the book *Playful Parenting*. Here are a few of the book's ideas-- you might want to read the book yourself.

Children benefit from high expectations, especially the expectations of being a moral person and pulling their weight in the family. Children need firm, clear limits. They may either feel all-powerful or out of control—neither gives them confidence. All-powerful children are outraged at any reminder that they are not in complete control. Out-of-control children look at their parents and think, "If they are not in charge, then who is?" Limits need to be given lovingly and respectfully, limits give structure, safety, and security to your children. This also helps them to feel safer about other dangers in the world. They want to feel the following: "My parents are powerful enough to keep me safe, until I can leave the nest and fly on my own, but not so powerful that I will never be able to test my wings."

You enter your children's world when you play with them; it is so important to play with your children, by doing that you learn who they are, and you can apply a playful discipline. When you play with them a closeness, some confidence, and a connection result when you enter their world. Children communicate, experiment, and learn when they play. Play is full of imagination. It forms a place in which children can fully be themselves. Play is fun, but also meaningful and complex. It is known that the more intelligent an animal is, the more it plays. Some of their learning happens automatically when they catch it, but much of it happens through play. Play is important and develops children. By playing with them.

you prevent many misbehaviors. Instead of punishing your children, turn the situation into a game and teach them how to behave.

When you play catch with your children, they are likely to enjoy it, and develop hand-eye coordination and gross motor skills. They will be able to practice a new skill and master it. The rhythm of the ball flying back and forth is a bridge that re-establishes a deep connection between parent and child. Your comments like "Good try!" and "Nice catch!" build confidence and trust. Many things happen when you play with your children of which you may not be aware. If they are constructively busy, not bored and have no time to get out of control, they will exercise, which is necessary for body and brain. Play builds closeness, it engages you with your children, and it pulls them out of emotional shutdown or misbehavior to a place of connection and confidence.

There is no end to the many ways you can use play to mend a relationship. To connect in love is very important-- we all need a full cup of love, closeness, and connection. It is a rich reward and a wonderful experience when you connect lovingly to your children. By playing with your children, you have fun, and you will also become aware of an improvement in your relationship with them.

Laughing together can make a connection, and making a connection often brings laughter. Laughter is healing and laughing together is a great way to let parent and child discover each other. It is important to work for improvement-- not to be perfect. Awareness and understanding do not mean you become perfect; you will still make mistakes. Remember to use kindness and firmness with your children. Kindness shows respect for them and their uniqueness. Firmness shows respect for the needs of the situation as well as your child's developing need to learn social skills. When you understand and respect your children's temperament, you can help them to reach their full potential as capable, confident, contented people. When you connect to your children, you will get more rest, laugh more, and learn a great deal about yourself and your children.

It may be helpful to know something about attachment and the developing child. Here are a few ideas about it.

CHAPTER 14

CREATE A LOVE FOR READING

Illiteracy is one of the biggest social problems in our world today. It must be terrible not to be able to read— one would miss out on so much. We don't teach our children to talk— we just talk to them. Learning to read happens in the same way. If a child hears the printed word read aloud to him, he will develop a curiosity to figure out the rules for reading, just as he figured out the rules for talking. They learn something more about reading every time you read to them.

Strickland Gillian says it so beautifully: "You may have tangible wealth untold: caskets of jewels and coffers of gold. Richer than I, you can never be-- I had a mother who read to me."

Some years ago, there was a survey taken among people who were well-known for both their achievements and for their community spirit. One of the questions was: "What childhood experience had the greatest influence on your life?" There were many different answers pertaining to nurturing and parental practices, but the most common response by far was, "My parents read to me!"

Reading and telling stories to your children have many positive effects. Stories can influence the way children think and behave because they like to hear them again and again. This repetition, combined with children's imaginations and the great power of a parent's presence, makes stories one of the best ways to influence children's thinking. It helps them to understand who they are.

Education is fundamental to who we are. Doctor Ben Carson, the neurosurgeon who grew up very poor, had a nickname in school— "Dummy." Raised in inner-city Detroit by a single mother with a third-grade education, Ben lacked motivation. He had terrible grades, and his pathological temper threatened to put him in jail. But Sonya Carson convinced her son that he could make something of his life, even though everything around him said otherwise. Though she herself couldn't read (and didn't let her sons know that she couldn't), Ben's mother had her boys read two books each week and write a report on each book. This inspiration made all the difference for Ben and his brother.

Trust in God, a relentless belief in his own capabilities, and sheer determination catapulted Ben from failing grades to the top of his class. He received a Yale scholarship and studied at the University of Michigan Medical School. Finally, at age 33, he received the Directorship of Pediatric Neurosurgery at Johns Hopkins Hospital in Baltimore, Maryland. Today, Dr. Ben Carson holds twenty honorary doctorates and is the possessor of a long string of honors and awards, including the Horatio Alger Award and induction into the "Great Blacks in Wax" Museum in Baltimore, Maryland. He is a God-fearing physician who lives to help others. Through it all shines a humility, quick wit, and down-to-earth style. In 2016, he even ran for President of the United States!

Thanks to Ben's mother, who never gave up, Ben has done great things with his life. His mother encouraged her sons to keep reading, and I want to inspire you to encourage your children to read as well. You can start reading very early in your child's life.

Your baby won't understand every word that you read to him, but he will grasp more than you realize. He will enjoy the cuddling, the sound of your voice and begin to associate books with pleasant feelings. I have read for hours to little Joseph, our only grandchild. He loves to listen and point out the things he sees in the book, and, when he plays, he often plays with those characters. Today, he is an avid reader who loves the written word!

Take your child on your lap and hold the book in front of him. Point to the words as you read. He will soon discover that you read from left to right and from the top to the bottom. He will also start asking questions about the words and the pictures that he sees. Select books that are appropriate for his age and for the values and other important matters that you would like your child to take in. Check the facts to make sure they are written correctly—especially Bible books. You can read the same book again and again to your children. They love to hear the stories repeatedly. Allow them to choose the book, and the library is available to all-- make good use of it. Reading has many benefits let us look at what reading can do for your children.

14.1   The advantages of reading

* Reading together bonds the child and the parent physically and emotionally. The physical contact gives the child a feeling of warmth and security. The shared stories usually lead to questions and comments by the child, which lead to meaningful conversations and emotional closeness. It builds relationship!

* Reading introduces the child to great literature and powerful stories, most with a moral message. Select classic stories that are well written and contain messages that focus on positive character traits. This gives them an appreciation and increases the possibility that they will be influenced by them!

* When parents read to their children, it fosters a love of reading. Research shows that children who are read to, are far more likely to read for both pleasure and information as adults. These children not only become better readers, but also develop their imaginations and become better-informed citizens!

* Listening when parents read, and when reading themselves, leads to success in school. Reading is inexpensive

entertainment; it helps meaningful conversations, moral lessons, and writing skills!

* Reading is your link with the world. It lets you share ideas, travel, learn, experience the joys and pain of others, and it enriches your life!

* Reading gives the child an understanding of the purpose of the printed word. Children develop a growing familiarity with written language that is essential to a successful experience with reading!

* Christians can nourish their faith in God's Holy Word. The biblical charge to raise a child in the ways of God carries a responsibility to raise a child who can read!

* *Reading has a wonderful way of calming restless children.* On a train, in a doctors' or dentists' offices, keep them busy by reading to them, or they can read themselves. Always keep a book in your bag!

* They can learn about emotions, people, Bible stories, trucks, etc. Young children have an enormous capacity for learning about different things. Create a love for reading about the topics that interest them.

* Children learn how to take care of books. Set an example how to handle books, and they will learn to take good care of books. Books need to be handled carefully as they are like friends.

* If they can read well, it can assist them with their homework. Every hour you spend reading together before he is five, is one hour you will not have to spend with your teenager on an assignment he cannot understand!

* By reading to your child, you are forming life-long patterns of learning. The first three years are the most important of forming life-long patterns of learning. Children understand more than you think!

* <u>Children learn language when you read to them.</u> They need lots of language input. They learn sentence structure, vocabulary, grammar, and much more!

* <u>You can identify a physical or health-related problem by reading to your child.</u> You can pick up a hearing or visual problem when you read and ask questions to your child. If you can identify a problem early, it is better to solve a problem while he is still young.

* <u>Reading is an effective use of time for a child and everyone else</u>. You will never know what ideas, desires, knowledge, or understanding can kindle in the mind of a child through a book. Books inspire careers, change our thinking, and can even change the course of history!

* <u>Reading a book together gives adults and children a shared background and experience.</u> You can talk about it when you have a similar experience, or something reminds you of something you read together.

* <u>A huge benefit that comes from reading is the emotional value it has.</u> When children grow up with a love for reading, it can assist them when they have a problem. By reading, they can identify with the person in a book and get carried away with "that" person. They become part of the story, and they identify their problem with the situation in the book. The information in the book does not only become part of the cognitive information, but it also becomes part of their emotional action. It becomes part of their victory over their struggles and gives them a solution to their problems. It can assist them throughout their lives.

Promote reading to your children because it has many advantages and helps them to develop. Teach them to choose books that have the same values that your family has and encourage them to read. Be a model for them by reading yourself. Assist them in becoming critical thinkers about what they read.

14.2   How to create a love for reading

Researchers have always been fascinated by children who come to school already knowing how to read. Some teachers are delighted; some are annoyed. What many teachers don't realize is that children learn to read on their own.

To foster a reading habit, it is important that reading takes place in the home, and that it becomes a family lifestyle. The parents should be serious about their children's attempts to read, and they should read aloud regularly to their children. It is necessary to have a wide range of printed materials in the home, such as magazines, books of all kinds, and newspapers. Help your children to read road signs, labels, menus, instructions, information on the computer, the internet, and a thousand other writing that you can see.

You don't need degrees and diplomas; you don't need technology. You don't need to be remarkable or learned in education and psychology. You only need a willingness to be consistent, lots of patience, and a willingness to read to him. Reading to your child should be a shared pleasure and keep it a pleasure. Read to your child just before bedtime to help him relax. Small children are also fascinated with poetry. A love of reading is one of the best legacies you can give your child and one of the best assurances that he will succeed in the future. Read to your child, keeping it light, happy, and relaxed. Be happy and loving, and read frequently to them. The children who did best in preschool reading were those whose parents read to them at least 60 minutes every day.

CHAPTER 15

CREATE A LOVE FOR NATURE

Nature was Adam and Eve's lesson book. In the Garden of Eden, the existence of God was demonstrated, and His attributes were revealed in the objects of nature that surrounded them. Everything upon which their eyes rested spoke to them. The invisible things of God, even His everlasting power and divinity, were clearly seen, being understood by the things that were made.

"The heavens declare God's glory and the skies reveal His handiwork. Day after day, they speak to us, and, night after night, they reveal God's wisdom. They do not have to speak with words of sounds, yet their voice is heard everywhere, and their words reach the ends of the earth..." (Psalm 19:1-4). "By the word of the Lord were the heavens made and all the stars by the breath of His mouth. He collects the ocean waters as we collect water in a bottle and stores them in gigantic reservoirs" Psalm 33:6, 7.

There are so many wonders all around us— spend some time with your children outdoors and discover some of the wonders that God has blessed us with. Rachel Carson says, "If a child is to keep alive his inborn sense of wonder, he needs the companionship of at least one adult who can share it, rediscovering with him the joy, excitement, and mystery of the world we live in."

In his 2005 book, *Last Child in the Woods: Saving our Children from Nature-Deficit Disorder*, journalist and child advocate Richard Louv introduced the term "nature-deficit disorder" to characterize the long-recognized suite of problems that could be attributed to childhood isolation from nature. Louv believes that early experiences in nature profoundly influence a child's physiological, emotional, and social development. According to Louv's findings, children disconnected from the out of doors are very unlikely to be concerned about nature. Even worse, he notes, they grow into adults

131

with little or no interest in conservation or environmental stewardship.

If we want to cultivate some knowledge about and a sense of responsibility for nature, we need to begin at a very young age. Miss Carson's sensitive and effective approach stimulated many young children's curiosity and has helped them to love and understand nature. She encourages observing, listening, and exploring, but, most of all, enjoying the wonders of the natural world. She said what is beautiful and awe-inspiring can be dimmed and even lost before they become adults.

Bringing the wonders of nature into a child's realm is easy. Even the busiest city has creeping, crawling creatures and plants that bloom and bud. Venturing out to take a thoughtful look at the richness around us is a part of our heritage as guardians of the natural world.

Very young children do not have to be told how wonder-filled nature is. Their eyes follow the course of a butterfly with fascination. Watching a baby's first encounter with a flower or a furry pet shows their great excitement! Opportunities to touch green grass, watch a bird take off in flight, and see how the wind carries leaves this way and that will activate your children's natural curiosity.

Starting seeds in a pot or small garden and tending them can be a satisfying shared activity. Growing and then eating a few kinds of vegetables can be the beginning of an understanding of life cycles and the food chain that we are part of. Planting a tree together once a year is also fun and could become a family tradition.

Watching your child run barefoot in the green grass or across a sandy beach will show you just how much pleasure they experience. Children love to be in the woods. Short hiking trips into the wild will produce lifelong memories of the sights, sounds, smells, and sensations found there.

"The quieter and simpler the life of the child—the freer from artificial excitement, and the more in harmony with nature—the more favorable is it to physical and mental vigor and spiritual strength." (DA 74)

Children can be weather watchers. Keeping a weather and temperature chart and recording observations can help your child understand the rhythm of the seasons. Noticing what types of clouds precede certain weather events can be exciting.

Expanding your windowsill or backyard garden will give your child a chance to see that each plant has its own characteristics and that each grows at its own rate. Starting a compost heap to produce rich fertilizer can show the relatedness of all things and the positive impact humans can have on nature.

"He (Jesus) lived to bless others. For this He found resources in nature; new ideas of ways and means flashed into His mind as He studies plant life and animal life." (DA70)

First impressions are lasting impressions. Even babes in arms, birth to six months old, will respond with interest to the wonders of their natural environment. The first year or two of a child's life is a special time when the child looks to the parent for guidance in all areas of learning. Seize the moment to instill in your child an interest and a reverence for nature and our natural world which offers the child a gift that will last a lifetime.

Listen with your children to bird songs. As each bird gives its distinct call, simply say the name of the bird—varied thrush, grouse, towhee, robin, woodpecker... Invariably, children will be fixated in silence, concentrating on the attention we give to the sounds of nature. Beyond the learning experience, these can be precious moments, rewarding for both child and parent.

Many are the ways in which God is seeking to make Himself known to us and bring us into communion with Him. Nature speaks to our senses without ceasing. The open heart will be impressed with the love and glory of God as revealed through the works of His hands. The listening ear can hear and understand the communications of God through the things of nature. The green fields, the lofty trees, the buds and flowers, the passing cloud, the falling rain, the babbling brook, the glories of the heavens— all speak to our hearts and invite us to become acquainted with Him who made them all. (*Steps to Christ*, 85 EGW)

CHAPTER 16

LEARN ABOUT ATTACHMENTS

The central theme of Attachment Theory is that primary caregivers who are available and responsive to an infant's needs allow the child to develop a sense of security. The infant learns that the caregiver is dependable, which creates a secure base for the child to then explore the world. Children attach, and mothers bond—bonding.

Attachment Theory focuses on relationships and bonds between people, especially parent and child. Attachment is an emotional bond with another person. This attachment or bonding impacts that which continues throughout life. Keep infants close to their mother to improve their survival.

Psychologist, John Bowlby, illustrated by his research that children's development depends on a strong relationship with at least one parent or caregiver. A child's attachment influences his or her personal development. Small children form an emotional attachment to their mother; this gives them a sense of stability and security, which is necessary in learning to take risks to grow and develop. This attachment bond is a love relationship.

The attachment bond is the first interactive love relationship infants have with their mother. The mother-child attachment bond shapes the infant's brain— it has a profound influence on their self-esteem, expectations of others, and ability to attract and maintain successful adult relationships. It helps to build healthier, attuned relationships, and to communicate more effectively within these relationships.

God made little children in such a way that they could attach to their mothers and experience happy emotions: they experience fear, anger, sadness, happiness, love, and joy intensely. This emotional attachment that grows between babies and their mothers is the first interactive relationship. Furthermore, it depends so much on the mother's nonverbal communication. The bonding that children experience will determine how they will relate to others throughout life because this creates the foundation for all verbal and nonverbal communication in their future relationships.

The relationship between infants and their mother shapes the success or failure of their future intimate relationships and helps to maintain emotional balance. Children who experience confusing situations, who are easily frightened, and/or had broken emotional communication while they were small often grow into adults who have difficulty understanding their own emotions and the feelings of others. This can limit their ability to build and maintain successful relationships. These people do not like themselves, nor do they find satisfaction in being with others. They are unable to bounce back from disappointment, discouragement, or misfortune.

When Professor Harlow did the test with the monkeys and their wire (1958) mothers, he came to the conclusion that being fed by your mother is not what attaches you to her. Rather, it is consistent, close nurturing that matters in early relationships. The finding with the monkeys had a great impact on psychoanalyst, Bowlby, who is the father of Attachment Theory. In his books, he set the groundwork for a new vision of attachment and sketched the stages that attachment relationships go through. He stated that the beginnings of attachment occur within the first six months of a baby's life. The baby cries, gazes into his or her mother's eyes, smiles, and even grasps onto her finger. Babies explore ways that promote interaction and pave the way for their attachment to their mother. Research has shown that babies become attached, not only to a single person, but to a network of people. When their mother is not around, babies are happy to play with dad or someone with whom they are familiar.

Professor Alan Stoufe of the University of Wisconsin and his colleagues have done several studies that indicate that children who have secure attachment relationships as infants make better adjustments in many areas later in their life. They found that two-year-old infants who had secure attachments when they were babies had more advanced make-believe play, worked harder, and were more persistent when given new problems. At age four, children with a secure attachment as babies showed more empathy and had higher self-esteem than children who had problematic attachments. When children have a sound attachment in infancy, it gives them a great start, but it needs to continue; temporary attachment cannot carry children through life, and they still need to be treated sensitively and responsively.

Attachments develop early in life and are not set in stone. The lack of a secure relationship could cause infants to have more difficulties later in life; however, infants can still develop secure relationships with others, as they become available, or the infants become more responsive. At nine months, children can already interpret the meanings of the emotional expressions of their parents.

Bonding happens with the parent. It is an emotional connection that influences the relationship with the child. Attachment is something that happens with children; they need to know for certain that they can always get to their parents and that they will welcome them with open arms. This is the foundation of becoming a secure, autonomous character who will have special qualities later in life. Someone said, "We are discovering increasingly each day how dependent a child's developing brain is on its mother's positive, attuned and responsive care." The studies that researchers conduct help us to understand why some people have trouble in communicating with the most important people in their lives, have problems, and/or cannot cope.

Here is a brief outline of the four attachment styles.

16.1   Four attachment styles

These four attachment styles were outlined by Drs. Ron and Nancy Rockey in *The Journey* (A recorded presentation).

These four attachment styles are, the avoidant, the ambivalent, the disorganized, and the secure self. There are four questions that everyone asks at some time during their development:

1. "Am I worthy of love?
2. Am I capable of getting the love I need?
3. Are others willing to love me?
4. Are others reliable and trustworthy when it comes to meeting my needs?"

16.1.1   The Avoidant

The avoidant answers the first two questions positively and the last two in the negative. Wounds received in childhood cause the developing mind in these children to compensate for their lack of connection with their parents or caregivers by determining that no one outside of themselves is safe or trustworthy. These children develop this way of thinking because they are often turned away when they ask for comfort or safety. They have learned that neediness is weakness, and reaching out is met with hurt, shame, and rejection. These children struggle with emotional connections— closeness is hard to find because the trust, which should have been developed in the first year of life was not in place. Displays of affection are rare in these individuals.

16.1.2   The ambivalent

Children with an ambivalent attachment style answer the first two questions negatively and the next two questions positively. They feel they are not worthy of love or capable of getting the love, acceptance, approval, and attention they need. These children experience no affection and approval, even when they are joyous and/or independent. They look for a hero, someone to rescue them from a loveless world. They live in fear that they will never be good enough to receive acceptance. Fear is the driving force behind their thoughts, feelings, and actions.

These children experience their parents' communication as inconsistent and, at times, disturbing. These children cannot depend on their parents for attunement or connection. When children experience inconsistent availability and unreliable communication from their parents, they are not sure what to expect. This ambivalence creates a feeling of insecurity in the parent-child relationship, and this is transferred to the child's interaction with his or her larger social world.

With both avoidant and ambivalent attachments, children develop an organized approach to their relationship with their parents. They want to make sense out of their experiences. They try to adapt to their world and re-create forms of relationships. They use old adaptations in new situations with teachers, friends, and later romantic partners. They believe that the world is an emotionally barren place (avoidance) or emotionally unreliable and filled with uncertainty (ambivalence)

16.1.3   The disorganized attachment

Children with a disorganized attachment have been abused in their emotional development, frozen in fear, and confused about their attachments. They are unable to grow in faith, hope, and love. They remain emotionally at the age where the wounding took place, even though chronologically they may be much older. Abuse is anything parents do intentionally to prevent their children from developing the ability to follow rules, to live within limits, and to love and be loved. If parents demand obedience without a relationship with the child, it causes rebellion. In a home where there is psychological neglect, physical abuse, sexual abuse, incest or molestation, exposure to severe marital conflict, or addictive behaviors, the child will develop a disorganized attachment style. People with a disorganized attachment style feel trapped in a chaotic world, one of rapidly shifting emotions, impulsive behaviors, and confused relationships. In this disorganized attachment, all four questions are answered negatively. These children feel unworthy of love, incapable of having their needs met, and that others are not willing to meet their needs. They see others as abusive and feel that they deserve the abuse.

Children need to get close to their parents during a time of distress so they can be soothed and protected. In this situation, the child is stuck because there is an impulse to turn toward the very source of the terror from which he or she is attempting to escape. It is an unsolvable dilemma for the child who can find no way to make sense of the situation or develop an organized adaptation. The only response of the attachment system is to become disorganized and chaotic. When children live in a chaotic home where abuse takes place, and where there is no safe place, and no person in whom to confide, they develop a disorganized attachment style. They learn to shift their pain to some other part of their consciousness. These children tend to solve conflicts in fantasy or play. They learn to pretend or imagine a better world and, consequently, they slip away into a world of their own; they daydream. Because their responses are so unpredictable, they have a broken self and become adults who have difficulty controlling their emotions.

The disorganized person suffers from identity problems, emotional storms, physical arousal, identification with the aggressor, faulty assumptions, distressed relationships, and lack of trust. The most important factor to remember about the disorganized attachment style is that it comes from trauma and abuse in childhood. It is a combination of the avoidant and ambivalent attachment styles. In addition, the responses and behaviors thereof are intense.

Research has demonstrated that parents whose unresolved trauma or loss experiences have not been worked through have a high likelihood of acting out behaviors that terrify their children and result in disorganized attachment for their children. It is never too late to move toward making sense of your experiences and healing your past. Not only you, but your children will also benefit!

16.1.4 The secure attachment

A healthy attachment is called a secure attachment and comes from sensitive parenting. These children are able to answer all four questions positively. They feel they are worthy of love and capable of getting the love and support they need. They feel that others are willing and able to love them and are accessible to them when needed. These people are equipped to face challenges and handle risks. With secure attachment, children experience being connected to their parents in a way that enhances their sense of security that affords them a feeling of belonging in the world.

If parents regulate and help children learn to soothe themselves and calm down when they are upset, they will later be able to regulate their own emotions and say to themselves, "I can calm down." Parents need to illustrate relational warmth and thereby help their children to experience relationships as safe and warm. Make family life interesting; play games and enjoy fun activities together. Children should learn, within the family, how to express their experiences, thoughts, feelings, intentions, and physical sensations. Children should be taught to meet the various developmental challenges of their lives: how to self-motivate; how to deal with separation; how to get along with others; how to respect authority; how to develop spiritually; and how to live morally. Life is all about relationships: to have respect for others, develop spiritually, live morally, treat others better than yourself, love and be loved, and respect other people's feelings. Children need to learn how to negotiate conflict, how to agree and how to disagree, and how to compromise.

Children who are securely attached do better academically and enjoy learning. They are physically healthier and have fewer colds and fewer trips to the doctor. Socially, they are better equipped and make friends more easily and maintain these friendships. They are more emotionally stable and display fewer negative emotions and are more positive, are better behaved, and have fewer problems with authorities and fights with others. These children have emotional strength; they are not afraid of their own emotions or those of others. They accept challenges and take risks, stand firmly for what they believe in, and invest in others because they do not fear loss. These children are willing to seek and accept comfort in distressing times. They display a sense of trust in others and in God, they tend to be optimistic, and they take responsibility for themselves and do not blame others for what happens. They are courageous, and act in the face of fear when they determine what action is needed. It is true that they also have negative emotions, but do not remain despondent because they are resilient.

16.2   How small children see themselves

It is important to take note that children under the age of eight or nine see themselves as the center of the universe. They take the credit or blame for whatever happens around them. When their parents get divorced, they think they are the cause of it. If they or others around them are abused, they blame themselves for it. If things go well in the family, they take the credit for that. This is how we were designed. When children have developed language and can communicate, they move out of the center and become part of the system of support and encouragement for others. However, if these basic needs have not been met—in other words, if children have been abandoned, abused, neglected or shamed— they will remain self-centered.

Newborn babies rely completely on their mother to fulfill their basic needs for comfort, nourishment, loving contact, and connection. If they do not receive it, they may express these needs through rage. The mother is also the baby's connection to the outside world, but when she does not care for him or her, specifically at this critical period, with the necessary eye contact, touch, motion, milk, and smiles, attachment does not take place. Control becomes a major issue and is directly related to children's ultimate concept of survival. Nearly half of everything a person will learn in a lifetime is learned during the first year of life. That is why it is a critical message for the baby's future development.

A story of a child who did not attach to his mother during infancy follows.

16.3   A Story of an Unattached Child

"Imagine being so consumed by rage that you are compelled to destroy everything in your world. Imagine feeling such primitive fury that your behavior becomes more animalistic than human and imagine enduring these emotions and being only five years old." This story is found in the book *Don't Touch My Heart* written by Lynda Mansfield and Christopher Waldmann.

The story of Jonathan highlights and explains the far-reaching social implications of attachment disorder. Jonathan's young life began with a series of foster parents, and eventually followed him into an adoptive home. He had terrible inner struggles and secrets, and he realized that he was different. He imposed terrible pain on his new family, particularly his adoptive mother. Jonathan did not bond because of his early abuse. He did not attach to his mother or anyone else during infancy, and he had difficulty giving and receiving love. His response to others was based on fear and uncertainty because he never trusted anyone but himself, and he believed he had to stay in control of all situations.

Jonathan never knew his father, and his biological mother did not know how to take care of him. She was addicted to drugs and often left him alone. When he cried, she did not pick him up and hold him. Instead, she screamed at him to stop. Jonathan did not understand her words. Sometimes she ignored him.

Although Jonathan was just a baby, he was beginning to

understand that he could not depend on his mother for anything. When he was three years old, she left him with a friend and never returned. This friend hit him when he started to cry, and she then called the police to take him away. The Children's Protective Services placed him in a foster home with five other children. Jonathan screamed and hit them; because he felt angry inside, the anger stayed with him. His foster parents tried very hard to be patient with him, but they were worried that he would hurt one of their children seriously. His behavior worsened. When he was four years old, they asked the social worker to remove him.

Jonathan was then placed with a kind, older couple. He was the only child living with them. He tried to bury his anger deep inside and smiled his sweetest smile because he wanted them to love him. He was on his best behavior with his new family. One day, the social worker came and took him to the park where he met his mother; he ran straight to her arms. She cried as she held him and spent some time with him in the park. The social worker arranged for him to go live with her again. His foster parents packed his belongings, and they cried and were very sad that he had to go. He did not care that they were unhappy because he was going home to his mother, and that was all that mattered to him. He did not say goodbye to his kind foster parents. He was happy to be back with this mother. After some time, the mother's boyfriend came and asked, "Who is this child?" She told him that she was babysitting for a friend. They shut the bedroom door and Jonathan just stared at the closed door. He did not understand all this. The boyfriend came out of the bedroom and started touching him in private places, but, when his mother came out of the bedroom, he pushed him away. Jonathan tried to climb into his mother's arms, but she pushed him away. The two then went out to eat and left him alone in the apartment.

Time went by, but his mother was not to return until much later. He became hungry and looked in the kitchen for something to eat and found a bag of sugar that he started to eat. He felt empty and alone, and then he fell asleep on the kitchen floor. His mother and Pete, her boyfriend, returned later that evening, laughing and shouting, which woke Jonathan up. He crawled under the table and curled up into a ball and covered his ears to block the noise. Later a policewoman picked him up. They had found cocaine in the mother and boyfriend's possession and took them away. The social worker took him back to his foster parents, the older couple, who were very glad to have him back.

When he was five years, the older couple took him to preschool. At the preschool, he crawled under the table and cried, "I don't belong here. I don't belong anywhere!" He scratched the teacher when she tried to comfort him, and he growled at the other children when they looked at him. The foster parents were shocked because he was such a good child at home. He refused to make any friends; rather, his anger was his friend. As time went by, the foster parents realized that there was something not-quite-right about his "pleasantness." His eyes never smiled with his mouth and when he hugged them; the hug felt cold, and when he told them that he loved them, the words sounded hollow and empty. Their love did not seem to reach him, and he became a stranger to them. They asked the social worker to come and take him away. The couple cried when she took him away, but Jonathan never cried. She took him to the children's home where he would stay until they could find another home for him.

One day while at home, he left and started walking down the street. It was a busy street with lots of traffic racing in both directions. He heard honking horns, screeching brakes and these noises excited him. He heard a siren and he hoped there would be a huge fire raging out of control somewhere; he imagined people being hurt in the fire and thought that would be good. A policeman stood next to him, and he threw himself into the policeman's arms and shouted, "I had to run away from that terrible place, and I have nowhere to go!" He told the policeman terrible lies about all the boys in his room; when he got the boys into trouble, it made him feel powerful, important, and very special.

Once again, Jonathan was placed with a loving family. Jonathan felt like a package that was lost in the mail and did not belong anywhere. The new family welcomed him into their home. They had a son who was seven years old and a daughter who was three. Jonathan pushed his anger and frustration deep down inside of himself and smiled at this new family. He thanked them for allowing him to live with them. He convinced his new parents that he was the perfect child. This family adopted Jonathan; they believed they could provide him with the love and attention he needed to grow into a happy secure child. He always seemed so polite and eager to please. But, whenever they were not looking, a very different Jonathan emerged.

Jonathan always got the two biological children into trouble and then called the parents; this happened many times. At first, they believed him, but, later, they discovered it was Jonathan who did the wrong things, just to get them into trouble. He felt very proud of himself for getting the two children into trouble. This happened repeatedly. Jonathan thrived when he was causing problems. He also tried to hurt their dog and told them that the dog wanted to bite him. Jonathan's actions started to cause some concern to the parents because they noticed that he seemed to be consumed by anger.

They planned a birthday party for him on his sixth birthday. Later, they found all the toys that he had received as gifts were broken. Because of this and all his other angry signs, they decided to take him to a psychologist. When he was alone with the doctor, he told her terrible lies about the parents and how they mistreated him. She reported back to the family that he was a normal boy and there was nothing wrong with him.

The family tried their best to make Jonathan happy. The mother baked his favorite cookies, read his favorite books, played his favorite games, and spent special time with him. She thought that all this would make him feel loved. They went to the movies, played on the playground, and went for long walks in the woods nearby. They gathered rocks and feathers and did many wonderful things to ensure he felt very loved and cared for.

They continued the sessions with the psychologist until the doctor felt it was not necessary anymore. However, one day the Children's Protective Services knocked on their door. They said that they had received an allegation of child abuse against them. The social worker said, "Jonathan says you are not feeding him, you never give him lunch money, and that you often send him to bed without dinner." The social worker added that he had begged her not to contact them, claiming that they would beat him for telling on them. She said he was very convincing in the stories he told.

The mother's fear gave way to anger, and she told the social worker that all this was not true, that he was a troubled child and had made up these stories. She said she had tried everything to make things pleasant for Jonathan, but it was as though he felt the need to distance himself from the rest of the family and his accusations filled that need. When they confronted him about his accusations, he said, "I am sorry I made up those lies. I do not know why I did it. Can you forgive me?"

The mother tried as hard as she could to help Jonathan to fit in with the family, but nothing seemed to work. He was still mean to their two children. He was rude to everyone he met, and his schoolwork began to suffer. The more the mother tried to please him, the worse his behavior became. He lied all the time. He stole food, money, things he already had, things that he did not need, things that he could not use, and he did not know why. Jonathan was having a good time. He knew that he had every member of the family under his control, and it was an intoxicating feeling to him. He burned their barn down with matches that he stole from a restaurant. The more the mother tried to help him, the more he misbehaved. In place of love, there was an anger growing inside Jonathan. His parents were very sad. They realized there was something very wrong with Jonathan.

His adoptive mother called the social worker and explained all these things to her. The social worker then asked them some questions and then explained that Jonathan had been subjected to neglect and abandonment throughout his early years; he behaved in ways that are very controlling, which prevented him from getting too close to others, and the distance made him feel safe. This problem is called attachment disorder because the child did not attach (bond) during infancy. The child's basic needs during infancy had not been satisfied, Jonathan's lack of attachment led him to believe that he could not count on or trust anyone. Fortunately, they found someone to help him who had knowledge about this disorder— but it was a very long road to recovery.

Learn as much as you can. Read, watch, listen, observe, and learn to understand your children. There is no greater challenge than parenting— however, there is also no greater reward than parenting! Look for the good in your children. Find alternatives to criticism and punishments. Focus on catching them being good and encourage and communicate appreciation— because they are wonderful! They are a gift from Heaven. Create a beautiful family with lots of laughter, play, and encouragement.

Remember discipline is a lifelong journey, it is not a technique. There is no success recipe for it— it simply is— AN ACT OF LOVE!

CHAPTER 17

CONCLUSION

Discipline is teaching and learning. Above are a few ways to teach and guide your children and keep them from becoming bored. When children are bored, they usually act out and get into trouble. Your most important work is to raise your children with love and respect! You need to inform yourself with as much knowledge as possible and you cannot do it alone. You need God's help to assist you and you need lots of prayer to raise them. Parenting is a relationship of love!

We are miracles of God. Every parent and every child is different, and we are all continually influenced by others. Every brain is wired differently, and we all react differently to the same situation, but our differences do not have to be challenges. We are all unique— God made us special!

In his book, *The Gardener and the Carpenter,* Dr. Gopnik states that, instead of thinking about caring for children as a type of work, aimed at producing smart, happy or successful people, we should think of it as a kind of love. He explained that love has a purpose, caring for our children is like tending a garden, and being a parent is like being a compassionate gardener. A successful gardener tends each plant with great love and care as he raises his flowers and vegetables. He gives them the best fertilizer or compost. During the cold winters, he protects them from the cold and frost, he protects them from insects, and he nurtures each plant so it can flourish. Plants do not always turn out the way you want them to, but plants can surprise you. They give you lots of pride and pleasure. Plants can be dynamic, variable, and resilient. Gardeners can lay a solid foundation so that plants can grow well and thrive. You need good soil and good seeds to grow beautiful flowers or vegetables. Just like the gardener, parents need to provide love and care for their children. Parenting can be wonderful and rewarding, but it can also be challenging and, at times, unpleasant and even overwhelming. Fortunately, there is a great deal of information available for parents so that they can raise well-behaved, healthy, and happy children. Good advice can make parenting a little easier. However, there are no guaranteed methods for ensuring that your children will be happy, healthy, and successful in life. Nevertheless, there is a plethora of research that reveals that dedicated parents can make a significant positive difference!

You are your child's first and most important teacher. Children learn constantly; they watch your actions and behavior. You must nurture, guide, protect and share with them. Young children are interesting and appealing, but they are also sensitive and vulnerable. Some days may be easy, but others may be a challenge. These variations are a normal part of raising a child. Maybe it would be easier if parents received some knowledge and training in what to do or how to do it. Unfortunately, children do not come with an instruction manual, and, even if there were one, there is no recipe for raising a child because each child is so different and so unique!

Parenting is a lot like receiving a job title without a job description, with no sick leave or vacation time, and you are put permanently on call every day, night, and weekend. The choice is yours to do much or little with your child. As with life, what you put into it—is what you get out of it. Try to learn all you can about your new job as a mother or father so that you can enjoy nurturing and teaching your child. You can get help by reading parenting books, attending parenting seminars, talking to family and friends, observing other parents, and, most importantly, praying to God for guidance. This is good advice because you cannot do it alone!

You have life's most important experience ahead of you when you raise a child and you may experience a wide range of feelings: joy, wonder and excitement, but also frustration, confusion, anxiety, sadness, and exhaustion. These feelings are very normal, but they cannot even be imagined, much less truly felt, without having a child. From the very first moment you hold your child, your world changes forever! Parenting must be learned and perfected through practice; when you become a parent, you will have plenty of experience and practice.

Appreciate and admire your children's unique qualities and discover their special needs, strengths, moods, and personality. Show them you love them! A showering of love means more than just saying, "I love you." Your children cannot understand what the words mean unless you treat them with love. You need to touch, cuddle, hug, talk, play, and sing to them. By touching them lovingly, you are stimulating them intellectually, a process that happens in the brain.

Your children will adopt some of your habits, so always be an example to them, and be responsible, loving, and consistent. Demonstrate how deeply you hold your beliefs and practice what you preach. It is important that you take good care of yourself. The healthier and happier you are, the better it will be for everyone. Remember, you are the most important person in your child's life, and no one can ever take your place!

Children learn to appreciate themselves as well as others from their parents. You show them how to love, trust, talk, laugh, play, and enjoy learning and living. Remember that the first three years of their lives are very important for everything that follows. During these years, you lay the foundation for the rest of your child's life.

Establish guidelines and routines, giving them responsibilities and rules that are appropriate for each phase of their development and adjust them as they grow older. By guiding, and lovingly disciplining and teaching your children, you will notice how they become increasingly independent. Any new skill requires work and practice. When, for example, you learn to play tennis, you need knowledge and tools. You need to practice until you have mastered various skills and, before you qualify to play at Wimbledon, you will need lots of practice and possibly a professional coach who can help you with the finer aspects of the game. This is how it is with parenting. It is not something you are but, rather, who you become with practice. You need to do it with intention and a purpose in mind. You do not have to be perfect. However, if you are the best you can be, God will be your helper.

Think for a moment, just after birth, your baby's brain contains billions of neurons. They are like the stars in the Milky Way. But when your child is eight, he will have many fewer than he has now. This sounds very destructive and not too productive. – But think of your child's brain as a block of marble in Michelangelo's hands, before he begins to work on it. Think of the same block of marble after he has transformed it into **a wondrous work of art. When the artist finishes, he has less marble, but he has a masterpiece!**

God is still looking for someone today who will love Him and raise His children with love. After Adam and Eve sinned, they roamed the earth because they were banded from Eden, they must have often whispered to each other, "God is love."—We should have been dead, but God was merciful to us! When Noah came out of the ark and realized that they were the only people left on the earth, he may have said to his family, "God is love." —He saved us and kept us safe in the ark—We should have perished with all those others—we were sinners too, but God was gracious to us! "Surely — God is love!" When Jesus came to dwell among men, He who was God came down to us and became man. "He was the image of God, the image of His greatness and majesty, the outshining of His glory. It was to manifest his glory that He came to our world, to this sin darkened earth. He came to reveal the light of God's love— to be God with us.! "He came and showed us all that—God is love! We as parents need that love when we raise our children. Because we love our children. We need to raise them with love to survive in this world today. Love has healing power. The greatest words today are, "God is love." And discipline is an act of LOVE.

Timothy Jennings in his book "*The God-Shaped Brain*" says "Brain development start in the utero. Brain imaging has shown that, when you worship a vengeful God who abuses freedom, or a punishing god, your fear circuits grow stronger, and your prefrontal cortexes are damaged. The prefrontal cortexes are the brain regions where you experience love, empathy, and selflessness. Brain research has demonstrated that the kind of God you worship changes your brain. Only the worship of a God of Love brings healing." As you raise your children remember the healing power of love!

Remember discipline is a journey, a journey of love, it is not a destination or a technique, and there is no success recipe for it—it simply is—AN ACT OF LOVE that you bestow on your children! May God bless you in this awesome responsibility as you show your love to your children by raising them with an act of love! Think of the healing power of love . . . And God will find that one that He is looking for to bestow his blessings on abundantly!

ABOUT THE AUTHOR

Doctor Emilie van Wyk met her husband, Dr. Gerhard van Wyk at college where they graduated together. They got married on December 12, 1965. Emilie taught in primary and secondary schools for 25 years and was a school principal for 20 years. She has also been involved in pastoral ministry with her husband and supported him when he was a lecturer at the University of South Africa.

Emilie studied at a Christian college and became a teacher in 1966. She later continued her studies at the University of South Africa while working full-time and obtained a BA (1985), HED (1987), B.Ed. (1989) (honors degree in which she specialized in Gifted Child Education), M.Ed. (1996) and her D.Ed. in Education in 2001. She wrote her master's thesis on *The Preschool Child and Their Literary Experience* and completed her doctoral dissertation on *Positive Discipline– A new approach to Discipline*. She has attended a variety of courses to enrich her education, and she is also fond of reading and researching different topics. Furthermore, she is interested in and loves gardening and vegan cooking. In addition, she enjoys photography and scrapbooking, loves people, and often travels to experience new places.

Emilie and Gerhard have two happily married children: Charl, who is a neuro-radiologist and Nadine, who is a pediatric anesthesiologist. Both completed their fellowship at Harvard. The van Wyks are a close-knit family and enjoy doing things together. Emilie and her husband were registered counselors with The American Association of Christian

Counselors (AACC). They had a parent club for many years and have shared their knowledge on raising happy and capable children with many others. They are presently working for their non-profit organization to serve people in need and present topics in their respective fields of expertise.

God has led both of them and specifically, Gerhard in marvelous ways. Emilie was inspired to write the beautiful life story of Doctor Gerhard van Wyk: *Christ's Grace is Sufficient for Me*. She was the editor of the book, *Beautiful Women*. She has also written the following books on parenting: *Creative Parenting– If I could raise my children again; Physical Development of the Small Child; The Intellectual Development of the Small Child; Children's Essential Needs and Parents' Challenges; The Moral Development of the Small Child; Raising Your Gift, Beautiful Children, and God's Dreamer – The Story of Joseph.* Her primary interest was, and still is, raising happy and capable children. In these books, she has gathered information from many different experts that will guide you while you enjoy your children. Parenting is much easier when you enjoy your children and understand their needs.

You are welcome to visit their website: www.zoecomm.com

Made in the USA
Columbia, SC
09 June 2023

17814393R00091